NE Choices:

the results of a
multi-component drug
prevention programme
for adolescents

Martine Stead • Anne Marie Mackintosh
Douglas Eadie • Gerard Hastings

Centre for Social Marketing,
University of Strathclyde

Report prepared for the Home Office

ACKNOWLEDGEMENTS

Our thanks go to the pupils and staff at the participating schools for their patience and co-operation throughout the research. We are grateful to Fiona Young, Tony Regan, Dave Bowditch and Bob Martin from the Drugs Prevention Advisory Service, North East Regional Office, Jayne Moules, formerly of the Northumbria Drugs Prevention Team, Tony Harrington and colleagues from Northern Stage, Fairbridge Tyne and Wear, the statutory and voluntary youth services and members of the NE Choices Liaison Group for their assistance. Thanks are also due to our interviewing team – Oria Farrage, Joan Suggitt, Margaret Vickers and Lilian Currie – and Susan Anderson from the Centre for Social Marketing and Jane Reece formerly of the Centre for Social Marketing for conducting and overseeing the survey fieldwork. In addition we would like to express our thanks to Margaret Jackson, formerly of the Centre for Social Marketing for her assistance with the qualitative research.

Finally, we would like to express our gratitude to staff, both present and past, at the Home Office Drugs Prevention Advisory Service HQ particularly Paul Baker, Tom Bucke, Charlie Lloyd and Teresa Williams for their help and guidance in producing this report.

Anne Marie MacKintosh
Martine Stead
Douglas Eadie
Gerard Hastings

Contents

EXECUTIVE SUMMARY

'NE Choices' is a multi-component drugs prevention programme for young people in the north-east of England. A previous report (Stead et al 2000) described interim findings from the first year of the programme with Year Nine secondary school pupils. This report describes the development and implementation of the second two years of NE Choices – the Year Ten and Year Eleven interventions – and reports findings from the evaluation of the full programme. The three-year intervention combined drama, work with parents, classroom activity, youth work, media and information activities. Pronounced 'any choices', the name captured both the programme's regional identity (NE = the north-east) and the concept of personal choice in relation to drug use, a central programme message.

TARGET POPULATION

NE Choices was targeted at a cohort of young people as they progressed through school between the ages of 13 and 16. There were three intervention phases:

- *Year Nine intervention* – delivered in 1996/97 to a target group aged 13-14.

- *Year Ten intervention* – delivered in 1997/98 to a target group aged 14-15.

- *Year Eleven intervention* – delivered in 1998/99 to a target group aged 15-16.

AIMS

The behavioural outcomes sought by NE Choices for young people were:

- to reduce the prevalence of drug use.

- to delay the age of onset of drug use.

- to reduce the frequency of drug use among those who use drugs.

- to reduce mixing of drugs including drugs and alcohol.

THEORETICAL BACKGROUND

NE Choices was based on the "social influences approach" to drugs prevention. Social marketing principles and techniques were also used to develop the programme, to ensure that it was acceptable and appropriate to all its target groups, delivery agents and intervention partners.

EVALUATION

NE Choices was evaluated at a number of levels.

- *outcome evaluation* – a longitudinal quasi-experimental study examined the attainment of behavioural outcomes. A baseline and three annual follow-up surveys were conducted with a cohort from six intervention and four control schools.

- *impact evaluation* – monitored the immediate response of the primary target group (young people) to key intervention components in terms of recall, participation, enjoyment, involvement, credibility and perceived messages.

- *process evaluation* – assessed the implementation of the programme, examining the consistency and integrity of delivery across sites, intervention reach, and responses to delivery among target groups and intervention partners.

- *formative research* – used throughout the programme to inform the design and execution of key intervention components.

DELIVERY OF THE YEAR TEN AND YEAR ELEVEN INTERVENTIONS

A range of integrated intervention components were designed and delivered in the second two years of NE Choices. The main components were:

- an all-day out of school drama workshop for Year Ten pupils.

- classroom support and follow-up, to reinforce the drama workshop.

- six month-long youth work projects, for Year Eleven pupils.

- an intensive outdoor activity programme for 'high risk' young people, in Year Eleven.

- drama sessions and drugs awareness sessions for parents.

- training for teachers, youth workers and school governors.

The main components in the Year Ten intervention were delivered as planned and attained a high reach – 94% of Year Ten pupils participated in the out of school drama workshop. The ambitious nature of this multi-media workshop posed organisational and resource challenges, but offered more control over delivery consistency, as well as an engaging experience for young people (see below).

The classroom follow-up was more intensive and co-ordinated than in the Year Nine intervention, reflecting a greater input from Northumbria Drugs Prevention Team (NDPT) in the form of a training programme and Teachers' Manual. The teacher training course and manual appeared to have increased teachers' knowledge and confidence regarding their ability to address drugs issues in the classroom. However, there were substantial variations between schools, and between teachers within schools, in the amount and type of follow-up that was delivered. This suggests that there are limits to the consistency of school intervention delivery that can be achieved, even when interventions are supported by standard training materials.

A substantial difference between the Year Eleven programme and previous interventions was in the design of the core interpersonal component for the primary target of young people. The Year Eleven interpersonal component comprised six unique youth-led projects. This meant that the intervention messages, themes and methods were more diverse than in previous years. The projects also involved far smaller numbers than the Years Nine and Ten interventions, with 44 pupils across the six evaluation schools completing projects. However, evaluation of the youth work component suggested that the involvement of the project participants was far more intense than in previous years. All groups met for several months, and the smaller size of the groups meant that participants' quality of interaction and learning was greater. A further 1,000 or so pupils participated indirectly, through either activities run by the project members or by receiving materials produced by the projects.

The 'high risk' programme was successfully implemented with eight young people – fewer than the intended 36 – and comprised outdoor activities, confidence building activities, a residential trip and drugs education. The parents' sessions were delivered as planned, but attracted small numbers. Training was delivered as intended to all key worker groups.

RESPONSE TO THE YEAR TEN AND YEAR ELEVEN INTERVENTIONS

The impact survey found that pupils reacted extremely positively to the Year Ten drama workshop. Pupils enjoyed the experience and found the actors and facilitators credible and engaging. High levels of emotional and intellectual involvement with the workshop were found, and pupils were stimulated to think about the different consequences of drugs and their own choices and attitudes towards drugs. Parents who attended the drama sessions found the workshops thought-provoking and informative, and felt that they had been provided with helpful ideas for discussing drugs constructively with their children.

The main Year Eleven components were evaluated qualitatively, because of their small numbers and diverse nature. The youth work projects appeared to foster strong feelings of ownership and confidence, as well as developing specific skills such as drama, video-making and art. It is possible that learning from the projects will have longer-term indirect benefits that are disseminated informally beyond the life span of NE Choices.

Young people enjoyed the high-risk programme, and felt a sense of achievement and increased confidence, particularly from the outdoor activities. Following the course, most made positive decisions regarding future education and training opportunities.

THE OUTCOME EVALUATION

A baseline and three annual follow-up surveys were conducted to examine the potential impact of NE Choices on drug taking behaviour. The baseline and first two follow-up surveys were administered within school but the final outcome survey, conducted beyond school year eleven, was administered by post to enable it to capture responses both from pupils who remained at school and those who left school after year eleven. Sample attrition, and possibly the change to a postal methodology, seemed to have the effect of reducing reported lifetime drug prevalence at the final survey. It seems that non-respondents at the final survey were more likely to have experimented with drugs, done so more frequently and initiated experimentation at a younger age.

Respondents' reluctance to disclose information that could potentially identify them resulted in difficulty matching responses between survey stages. Only 54 percent of the original sample could be matched to the final survey. The report presents data from both cross-sectional and matched (longitudinal) analysis.

Cross-sectional analysis examined young people's exposure to drug offers. There was access to a range of drugs, particularly cannabis. Over half had experimented with drugs. Cannabis was the main drug to have been tried although many had tried amphetamines, nitrites, solvents, LSD and magic mushrooms. A minority of experimenters, peaking at a fifth, had, in the six months prior to the survey, taken more than one drug at the same time. Taking drugs in combination with alcohol was more prevalent with nearly half the experimenters having done so. Drug taking behaviour seemed to be consistent across the different levels of intervention. There did not appear to be any evidence that NE Choices had impacted on drug prevalence or harm reduction as intended.

The cohort of respondents who could be matched between baseline and the final follow-up survey were not representative of the original baseline respondents and, for example, under-represented prevalence of drug experimentation, smoking and weekly drinking. However, they provided an opportunity to examine transitions in and out of drug taking status. Over half remained non-triers of drugs between the baseline and the third follow-up, while over a fifth (22%) progressed into drug experimentation or use. There is evidence of a de-escalation of drug use in a very small proportion – two percent – that is, people no longer using certain types of drugs when questioned. Progression of drug taking did not vary by intervention level but respondents from full intervention schools reported the highest level of de-escalation from drug use. While the numbers and proportions were small the data suggests that, within the matching cohort, NE Choices may have encouraged full intervention respondents to de-escalate drug use, by changing from harder drugs to cannabis, solvents or nitrites or to non-use. However, it is not possible, due to the level of matching, to identify whether or not the full sample showed the same transition in their drug taking.

CONCLUSIONS

Despite compelling evidence that young people found NE Choices credible and engaging, the intervention was not associated with any changes in drug taking behaviour. A number of possible explanations are discussed including methodological issues, intensity of delivery and appropriateness of the target group. NE Choices may have been insufficiently intensive, being less intensive than some major US-based interventions, and 11 may have been a more appropriate age than 13 for pupils at the start of the intervention. Other possible explanations are that the intervention had an inappropriate theoretical basis, was poorly or inappropriately implemented; was not sufficiently different from the drugs education delivered in comparison schools, and did not sufficiently involve the community. Finally, a number of recommendations regarding future drugs prevention practice and research are identified.

ABOUT THIS PAPER

The remainder of the paper contains eight sections. Chapter 1 describes the theoretical basis, origins, development and design of the programme. Chapter 2 outlines the evaluation methodology. Chapter 3 presents findings from the process evaluation concerning delivery of the Year Ten and Year Eleven interventions. The reactions of young people and teachers to the Year Ten intervention are examined in Chapter 4. Chapter 5 reports on the reaction of young people, youth workers and parents to the Year Eleven intervention. Chapter 6 presents cross-sectional data on drug offers and drug-taking and Chapter 7 presents longitudinal findings from the outcome evaluation for the matched cohort. Chapter 8 discusses the conclusions.

1. DESIGN, ORIGIN AND DEVELOPMENT OF NE CHOICES

1.1 DESIGN OF NE CHOICES

Overall Design

NE Choices was a three-year multi-component drugs prevention programme implemented by Northumbria Drugs Prevention Team (NDPT). Multi-component programmes use multiple channels to deliver an integrated programme of activities and messages to promote behaviour change, and have been found to be more effective than those using a single channel (e.g. Klepp et al 1993, Perry et al 1992). For example, tobacco and drugs prevention programmes which combine school-based activity with mass media activity have had a more favourable effect on behaviour than those comprising school or media activity alone (e.g. Flynn et al 1992, Johnson et al 1990, Pentz et al 1989, Pentz & Valente 1993). NE Choices delivered the following integrated mix of programme components to provide comprehensive and consistent drugs prevention messages and support for behaviour change:

- interpersonal components: drama workshops, classroom activities, sessions for parents, youth work projects and intensive work with high-risk youth.

- information products: magazines, reference files, website, computer software, and teaching and policy manuals.

- community awareness and support activities: Unpaid publicity through the local media, consultation with community leaders, and drugs awareness support to local community groups.

Figure 1.1 summarises the mix of different components delivered in each year of the intervention. The three intervention years were labelled 'Year Nine', 'Year Ten' and 'Year Eleven' to reflect the school year in which the primary target group was exposed to phases of the intervention. The intervention content is discussed in more detail later in this section.

Figure 1.1: NE Choices – intervention content over three years

January 1997–

> **Year Nine Intervention**
>
> ***Age of target group***:   13-14
>
> ***Intervention components:*** Drama workshop, 'Friday Forum', classroom follow-up, parents' sessions, information products, media activity, school governor training, school support, community consultation.

April 1997

January 1998–

> **Year Ten Intervention**
>
> ***Age of target group***:   14-15
>
> ***Intervention components:*** Out of school drama workshop, teacher training and manual, classroom follow-up, information products, media activity, school governor training.

April 1998

August 1998–

> **Year Eleven Intervention**
>
> ***Age of target group***:   15-16
>
> ***Intervention components:*** Peer-led youth work projects, youth and community worker training, intensive residential and follow-up intervention with 'high risk' youth, parents' workshops, information products, media activity, school governor training.

March 1999

Theoretical Basis of NE Choices

NE Choices adopted a behavioural approach to drug use based on the 'social influences' model. More information on the social influences approach is provided in the previous DPAS report on NE Choices (Stead et al 2000).

NE Choices differed from other social influences programmes in some aspects.

- *The target group was slightly older.* The NE Choices 13–16 target group was slightly older than the typical 10–14 target for many social influences programmes (e.g. Gropper et al 1995, Ellickson et al 1993a, Ellickson et al 1993b, Botvin et al 1990, Botvin et al 1995, Pentz et al 1989, Pentz & Valente 1993). The transferability of the approach to an older target group was unproven.

- *The programme had broad aims.* Social influences programmes tend to focus solely or primarily on prevention (e.g. Pentz et al 1989, Elder et al 1993 and 1994, Botvin et al 1990 and 1995). NE Choices did not aim solely to prevent and delay onset of drug use, but also aimed to reduce harm. There has been less evaluation of the effectiveness of the social influences approach in the context of harm reduction.

- *The programme used actors as key delivery agents.* Many of the evaluated social influences prevention programmes have been school-based, using a curriculum or package delivered by teachers (e.g. Botvin et al 1990 and 1995, Ellickson et al 1993a). NE Choices utilised actors and youth workers to deliver core components, with teachers following up this work in the PSHE curriculum. The relative merits of different delivery agents (i.e. classroom teachers versus external agents such as actors or youth workers) is a debated issue (e.g. Blakey & Pullen 1991). However, drama-based interventions have been recognised as powerful media for addressing sensitive issues such as drugs, safer sex, HIV/AIDS and alcohol use (Wragg 1990, Denman et al 1995 and 1996, Wilmott 1996). They can present difficult issues non-threateningly through the lives of fictional people, who act as a vehicle through which the audience can project and explore different opinions and experiences (Blakey & Pullen 1991). They can also trigger discussion and "act as a catalyst for opening channels of communication" between young people and adults (Blakey & Pullen 1991, p161).

- *The programme was smaller in scale.* Compared with several of the social influences programmes discussed above, NE Choices was smaller in scale, of shorter duration, and less intensive (eg. Botvin et al 1990 and 1995, Pentz et al 1989, Johnson et al 1990). This raised the question whether the NE Choices programme was substantial enough to produce intervention effects.

Target Groups

NE Choices had a primary target of 13-16 year olds, and secondary targets of parents, teachers, school governors, the media and the local community.

The Year Nine and Ten interventions, delivered in the first and second years of NE Choices, were *universal* in coverage, targeting all same-age pupils in each participating school. The Year Eleven intervention contained both universal and selective coverage elements. *Selective* interventions are targeted on sub-groups, such as those considered at high risk of drug use or problematic drug use.

Programme Aims

The behavioural outcomes sought by NE Choices for young people combined both prevention and harm reduction:

- to reduce the prevalence of drug use.

- to delay the age of onset of drug use.

- to reduce the frequency of drug use among those who use drugs.

- to reduce mixing of drugs including drugs and alcohol.

Combined prevention and harm minimisation aims were considered appropriate for the 13-16 year old age group, a proportion of whom were likely to be already experimenting with drugs by age 13-14 (e.g. Barnard et al 1996, Newcombe et al 1995, Miller & Plant 1996, Parker et al 1995).

Programme Messages

The programme avoided overt abstinence messages, instead emphasising the themes of understanding the consequences of different choices concerning drug use, making informed choices, and on taking responsibility for these choices. The name 'NE Choices' reinforced this message.

To influence perceptions of social norms concerning drug use and reduce exaggerated perceptions of peer use, NE Choices sought to convey messages that 'not everyone is taking drugs'. The programme also conveyed the message that it is possible and acceptable to step back from occasional experimental use (Home Office Drugs Prevention Initiative 1998), by depicting fictional characters who chose not to continue using drugs after one-off experimentation.

Specific harm reduction messages were also incorporated, concerning the effects of mixing drugs and alcohol, the risks of other poly-drug use, how to reduce harm when taking drugs and how to cope with an emergency situation.

Social Marketing

Social marketing theory and practice (Kotler & Zaltman 1971, Andreasen 1994, Kotler & Roberto 1989) was used to guide development, organisation and implementation of the programme. Social marketing emphasises the importance of consumer orientation – that is, ensuring that 'product offerings' (in this case, the drugs prevention programme) are appropriate and acceptable to all groups involved (Hastings & Haywood 1991). By this is meant not only the ultimate recipients of the programme, the young people, but also those agencies and individuals charged with the responsibility of delivering it. The programme demonstrated its commitment to this principle by undertaking, in 1996, a programme of formative research and a full one-year pilot of the intervention (see also Section 2.4 below). Social marketing also brings to behaviour change programmes the concept of beneficial exchange (Bagozzi 1975, Houston & Gassenheimer 1987) between intervention planners, target groups and other stakeholders, and stresses the importance of continuous and strategic formative and process research (Lefebvre & Flora 1988, Balch & Sutton 1997), audience segmentation and targeting (e.g. Andreasen 1995, Lefebvre et al 1995).

Intervention Content

As noted above, the content of the NE Choices intervention varied each year to reflect the changing needs and interests of the target groups. The Year Nine intervention comprised: an in-school drama workshop delivered to Year Nine pupils in their class groups; an information and discussion session for a smaller group of pupils acting as class representatives; some classroom follow-up work by teachers; sessions for parents; a range of media and information products; training for school governors, and support for schools in developing drugs policy. More information on the Year Nine intervention is provided in DPAS Paper 4 (Stead et al 2000).

The Year Ten intervention comprised an all-day out-of-school drama workshop at which Year Ten pupils, in self-selecting peer groups, embarked on an interactive quest to investigate the drugs-related disappearance of a female fictional character. The quest, which involved interviews and discussions with actors playing characters in the girl's life, was designed to encourage pupils to reflect on their own choices and beliefs about drugs. The workshop was followed up by an optimal four classroom sessions, led by PSHE or guidance teachers. To help teachers to implement this part of the intervention, teacher training, plus a manual of lesson plans and resources was provided. A range of high quality drugs information products, including a filofax-type Factfile for each pupil and a CD-Rom developed by the Health Education Authority, were used to reinforce these interpersonal components.

The Year Eleven intervention comprised three main components, each for different target groups. The first was a youth work programme attached to each intervention school for six months, with NDPT funding for staff, resources and activities. Within each project, a small group of volunteer Year Eleven pupils devised and produced their own choice of drugs education work (for example, a video, board game or drama) and displayed the work to their peers. The second component was parents' programme, comprising drama-based drug awareness sessions and support groups. The third component was an intervention tailored to the needs of young people deemed to be at particular risk of drug use and harmful drug use because of difficulties at school and home. This intervention component was designed and delivered by Fairbridge in Tyne and Wear, a charitable organisation that works with young people with social, behavioural and other difficulties. A number of other supporting components were developed and implemented, including training for youth workers involved in the projects, and information materials for parents on how to discuss drugs with their children.

Throughout both the Year Ten and Eleven intervention periods, other components that had formed part of the Year Nine intervention continued to be implemented. These included press and public relations activity, a revised and more interactive NE Choices website, a revised Family Fact File (an information file targeted at parents), and a revised Governor Fact File (an information file targeted at school governors).

Figure 1.2 summarises the full range of intervention components over Years Nine, Ten and Eleven. The rationale behind the design of the Year Ten and Eleven interventions, and the processes by which they were developed and delivered, are described in section 3 below. As the Year Nine intervention is described in detail in DPAS Paper 4 (Stead et al 2000), its development and delivery are not covered in this report.

The table indicates, for each component, its intended target group, the agency or individuals who delivered or produced it, a brief description of content and format, and aims. The table also indicates whether each component was delivered to three schools receiving the full three-year intervention (full intervention schools) or to six intervention schools, three receiving a partial version (components for young people only) and three receiving the full programme. The delivery of different intervention levels is described in more detail in Chapter 2.

The Year Ten and Eleven interventions, like the Year Nine intervention, were delivered to all of the six schools participating in the evaluation. In addition, as in Year Nine, additional schools in the Northumbria area also received the intervention. This was because Northumbria Drugs Prevention Team made additional funding available to enable the intervention to be delivered in a number of schools in each of the six local authority areas in Northumbria. In Year Nine, 26 schools in total, including the six evaluation schools, received NE Choices. The Year Ten and Eleven interventions were more resource intensive, and therefore it was not possible to deliver these to all 26 of the original schools. Instead, 13 schools, including the six evaluation schools, took part in the Years Ten and Eleven intervention. This report focuses on the delivery of the intervention in the six evaluation schools, although some information on delivery in all 13 schools is provided.

Figure 1.2: NE Choices intervention components over Years Nine, Ten and Eleven

Component	Target group	Delivered/ produced by	Description	Aims
Year 9 Drama workshop	Year 9 pupils *All 6 evaluation schools*	Northern Stage theatre company	Two and a half-hour workshop in school comprising: • Play about a 15-year-old boy's first exposure to a drug (an offer of cannabis) and the consequences of him agreeing to buy more cannabis for his girlfriend. • 'Hotseating' in which pupils questioned the characters about their motives and feelings. • 'Forum theatre' in which young people roleplayed different choices the main character could have made.	Raise awareness of consequences of drug-use choices. Explore realistic behavioural choices young people can adopt in drug-offer situations. Allow young people to rehearse different strategies to deal with drug-offer situations.
Friday Forum	Year 9 pupils *All 6 evaluation schools*	Northern Stage theatre company	Two-hour session for representatives from each Year 9 tutor group, comprising information, group work activities and discussion.	Equip group with drugs prevention information for dissemination to peers informally or through classroom discussion.
Classroom follow-up	Year 9 pupils *All 6 evaluation schools*	Teachers	Content and approach at discretion of individual teachers. Teachers pack provided (see below).	Reinforce messages from drama workshop and encourage further discussion.
Parents' session	Parents of Year 9 pupils *3 full intervention schools only*	Northern Stage theatre company	Two-hour after-school sessions comprising a modified version of the drama workshop delivered to Year Nine pupils, information and discussion.	Raise parents' awareness, provide information and support, and encourage parents to reinforce intervention messages.
NE Choices magazine	Year 9 pupils *All 6 evaluation schools*	NDPT and Procter & Gamble	High quality magazine containing detailed information about use and effects of specific drugs, quizzes, advice, and problem pages.	Provide information and support in a credible, attractive format.
Teachers' pack	Year 9 teachers *All 6 evaluation schools*	NDPT and Procter & Gamble	Pack of ideas and material for drugs education activities linked to the themes, approach and content of the drama workshop.	Provide information and support to teachers following-up the drama workshop in class.
Community mapping	Community *All 6 evaluation schools*	NDPT	Mapping of existing community groups and parent networks in the communities served by the evaluation schools.	Identify appropriate channels for promotion of intervention to parents.
Years 10 & 11 Drama workshop	Year 10 pupils *All 6 evaluation schools*	Northern Stage Theatre Company	Full day out-of-school workshop at Discovery Museum, Newcastle upon Tyne city centre. Pupils worked in groups to investigate disappearance of fictional character, interacted with actors playing characters in her life and used computer software to explore aspects of drug use.	Develop understanding of personal and social consequences of drug use. Explore realistic choices, including harm reduction, which young people can adopt in drug offer and use situations.
Classroom support and follow-up	Year 10 pupils *All 6 evaluation schools*	Teachers	Four classroom sessions building on the themes and information communicated in the drama workshop, using the Teachers' Manual (below).	Reinforce messages from drama workshop and encourage pupils to explore issues in greater depth.

Component	Target group	Delivered/ produced by	Description	Aims
Youth work projects	Year 11 pupils *All 6 evaluation schools*	Statutory and voluntary sector youth workers	Six-month youth work projects attached to schools. Participants engaged in various confidence and skill-building activities, and devised a drug education 'product' for delivery to their peer group at the end of the 6-month period.	Develop young people's peer education skills (e.g. communication, art skills). Enable young people to develop and disseminate a tangible drug education product.
Interactive exhibition (Video Box)	Year 11 pupils *All 6 evaluation schools*	Blackbox productions	Touring interactive exhibition and workshop featuring ideas from all of the youth work projects. Present in schools for 3-5 days each.	Extend the range of the youth work projects to a larger number of young people.
Parents' drama session	Year 11 parents *3 full intervention schools only*	Live Youth Theatre	Evening session including an interactive drama workshop about young people's drugs & alcohol choices, and discussion about parent-child communication about drugs.	Raise parents' awareness of drug issues and encourage positive, informed parent-child communication.
Parents' awareness session	Year 10 & 11 parents *3 full intervention schools only*	Local training consultants	Drugs awareness sessions facilitated by drugs trainers in informal settings in the community, at the request of groups of parents.	Raise parents' awareness of drugs issues.
High risk young people's programme	Year 11 pupils deemed high risk *All 6 evaluation schools*	Fairbridge	Intensive one-week long course involving outdoor activities aimed at building skills and confidence, tailored for young people identified as 'high risk' by schools. Followed up by individual support and guidance.	Build high-risk young people's confidence and skills. Raise awareness of consequences of drug use and explore safer drug use choices.
Teacher training	Teachers *All 6 evaluation schools*	NDPT	One-day training course for all Year Ten tutors involved in PSHE and guidance.	Develop teachers' drugs education knowledge and skills.
Youth worker training	Youth-workers *All 6 evaluation schools*	NDPT	Two-day training course for statutory and voluntary sector youth workers.	Develop youth workers' drugs knowledge.
Factfile	Year 10 pupils *All 6 evaluation schools*	NDPT and Procter & Gamble	Filofax-type product containing information about use and effects of specific drugs, information relevant to the drama quest, and pages for notes, addresses and a diary.	Provide information in a credible, attractive format. Reinforce Year Ten drama workshop themes.
CD-Roms	Year 10 pupils *All 6 evaluation schools*	NDPT, Sunderland University, HDA	D-Code CD (produced by the HDA, formerly HEA), CD of NE Choices website, and CD of interactive website produced to support the drama session at the Discovery Museum.	Provide drugs information in attractive interactive format, and extend life of NE Choices interpersonal components.
Teachers' Manual	Teachers *All 6 evaluation schools*	NDPT and Procter & Gamble	Durable resource manual containing lesson plans, worksheets and handouts.	Support teachers in delivery of classroom follow-up.
Media literacy materials	Teachers *All 6 evaluation schools*	NDPT	Curriculum materials for use in PHSE, English or media/communication studies exploring how drugs issues are portrayed in the media.	Encourage discussion of drugs issues by examining their portrayal in the media.

Component	Target group	Delivered/ produced by	Description	Aims
YEARS 9, 10 AND 11				
Family Fact File	Parents *All 6 evaluation schools* [1]	NDPT and Procter & Gamble	Durable reference file containing information about use and effects of specific drugs, sources of advice, the law, and suggestions for parent-child discussion about drugs.	Provide information in a credible, attractive, durable format.
Governor Fact File	School governors *All 6 evaluation schools*	NDPT and Procter & Gamble	Durable file containing information about specific drugs and issues to consider in a school drugs policy.	As above.
Governor Training	School governors *All 6 evaluation schools*	NDPT in partnership with local providers	Part of a wider school governor training initiative in Northumbria.	Raise drug awareness and encourage effective school policies for drugs education and incident management.
Websites	Year 9-11 pupils, general public	Sunderland University	Interactive websites containing material linked to the drama workshops and NE Choices magazines.	Provide information and support in interactive format.
Press and public relations	Local media, community	NDPT (Year 9), Batwatch (Years 10 & 11)	Press releases, editorial features, launches, participation in media interviews.	Raise community awareness of and support for the intervention.
Sponsorship & endorsement	Community	Various	Endorsement and in-kind sponsorship of the intervention was provided by Newcastle United and Sunderland football clubs, local rugby, basketball and ice hockey teams, and local celebrities Kevin Whateley and Ant & Dec.	As above.

[1] It was not feasible to restrict access to the Family Fact file to parents of pupils in the three 'full intervention' schools only, because it was distributed thhrough a telephone information line. The file was therefore available to all parents. However, it was more heavily promoted in the full intervention schools than in other schools

2.   EVALUATION METHODOLOGY

A full account of the methodology used to evaluate NE Choices up to the end of Year Nine is provided in a previous paper (Stead et al 2000). This section provides an overview of the evaluation methodology used over the full intervention period.

NE Choices was evaluated using an integrated research design (Hastings et al 1997) comprising *outcome evaluation, process evaluation, impact evaluation, and formative research*. The integrated research design was intended to:

- show the effects of the programme.

- provide possible explanations for outcomes achieved.

- highlight unforeseen consequences of the programme.

- identify lessons regarding programme implementation.

Other researchers have identified the benefits of 'mixed methods' evaluations in drug prevention (e.g. Gilham et al 1997). Integrated evaluations are of particular value in programmes that involve many types of delivery processes and potential changes (e.g. Fawcett et al 1997).

Figure 2.1 illustrates the relationship between formative, process, impact and outcome evaluation.

2.1 OUTCOME EVALUATION

The outcome evaluation used a longitudinal quasi-experimental study to determine whether the behavioural outcomes of NE Choices were met. Ten schools participated in the outcome evaluation. Six of these received the intervention and four were control schools (Table 2.1). The intervention schools were further divided whereby three schools received a full version of the Year Nine intervention (all components) and three received a partial version (components for the primary target group of young people only). The delivery of different intervention levels was intended to test the assumption that the components for the primary target group would have a greater impact if reinforced by components for secondary target groups such as parents.

Figure 2.1: Relationship Between Research Elements

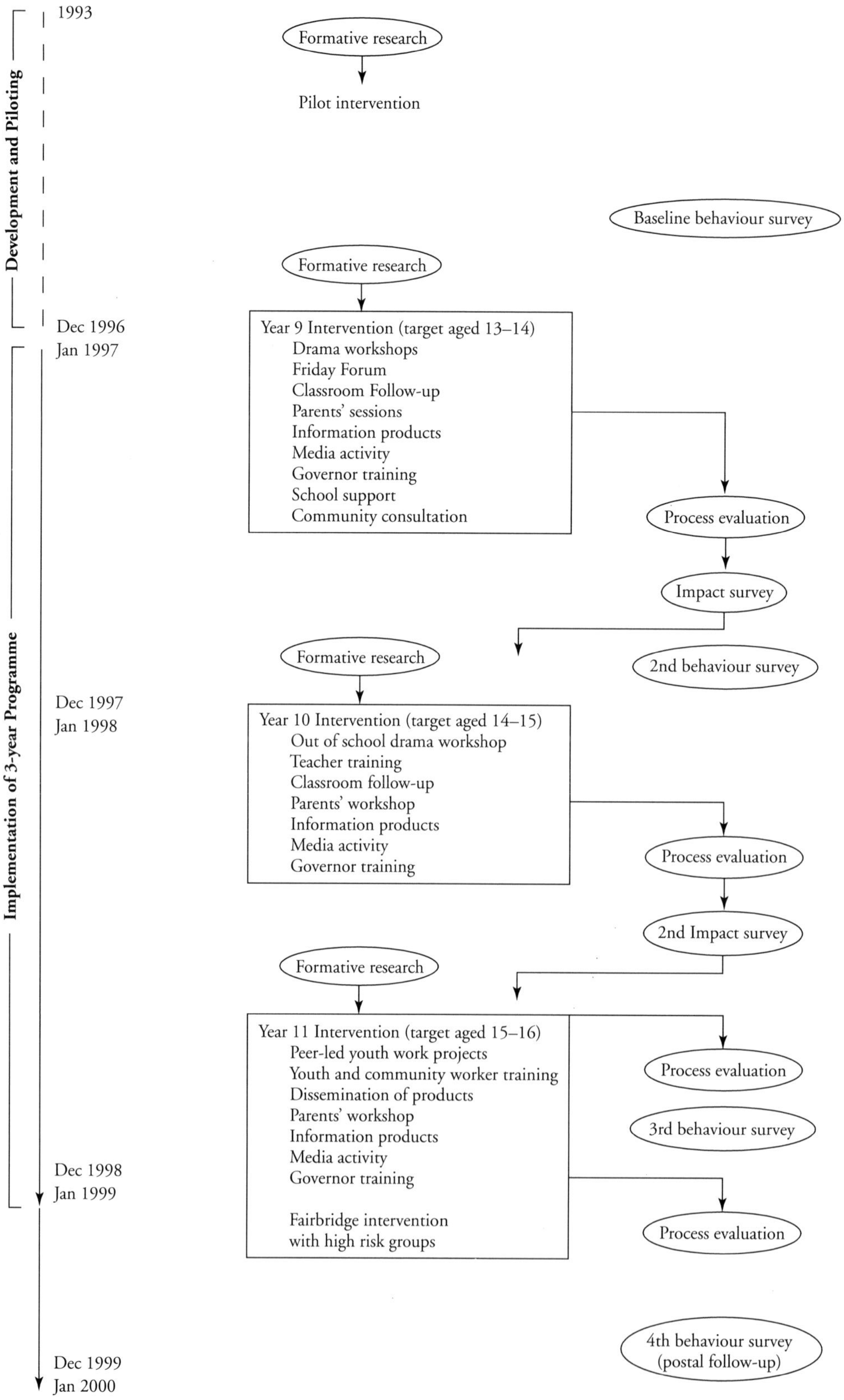

Development and Piloting

1993

Formative research

↓

Pilot intervention

Baseline behaviour survey

Formative research

↓

Dec 1996
Jan 1997

Year 9 Intervention (target aged 13–14)
    Drama workshops
    Friday Forum
    Classroom Follow-up
    Parents' sessions
    Information products
    Media activity
    Governor training
    School support
    Community consultation

Process evaluation

↓

Impact survey

2nd behaviour survey

Implementation of 3-year Programme

Formative research

↓

Dec 1997
Jan 1998

Year 10 Intervention (target aged 14–15)
    Out of school drama workshop
    Teacher training
    Classroom follow-up
    Parents' workshop
    Information products
    Media activity
    Governor training

Process evaluation

↓

2nd Impact survey

Formative research

↓

Year 11 Intervention (target aged 15–16)
    Peer-led youth work projects
    Youth and community worker training
    Dissemination of products
    Parents' workshop
    Information products
    Media activity
    Governor training

    Fairbridge intervention
    with high risk groups

Process evaluation

3rd behaviour survey

Dec 1998
Jan 1999

Process evaluation

Dec 1999
Jan 2000

4th behaviour survey
(postal follow-up)

Table 2.1: Allocation of School to Intervention

Number of schools	Experimental Status	Intervention Components Received
3	Experimental: Full Intervention	All intervention components
3	Experimental: Partial Intervention	Components aimed at primary target of young people
4	Control	None

Four surveys, monitoring behaviour in relation to drugs, were conducted with a cohort of pupils in each school. The first survey, a baseline prior to implementation of NE Choices, was conducted with the cohort of Year Nine pupils in Autumn 1996. The second and third surveys were conducted in Autumn 1997 and Autumn 1998 respectively. A fourth postal survey in Autumn 1999 followed up young people after they had left school.

Sampling Procedure

The intervention schools were selected using a multi-stage procedure. All schools in Northumbria (60 in total) were invited to participate in the intervention and evaluation. A total of 36 replies were received. Fourteen schools were eliminated at the first level of selection because they: were too small (12 schools having fewer than 200 Year Nine pupils); were participating in other drugs research (one school), or only provided education for a limited age group (one school). From the remaining 22 schools, a homogeneous sub-sample of nine schools of similar demographic composition (based on census data for the postcode within which each school was located) and academic achievement (OPCS 1994, DfEE 1995) was identified. Six schools were randomly selected and assigned, with stratification by academic achievement and demographic profile, to partial or full intervention status. Ideally, stratification by baseline level of drug use might have been preferable but such information was not available at the time of selection. Data on academic achievement and demographic profile were therefore used for stratification to ensure that full and partial intervention status contained a similar range of schools.

The control schools could not be drawn from Northumbria as the whole area was exposed to the media components and had the potential to buy into NE Choices. In order to eliminate any contamination between intervention and control schools, the control schools were drawn from the neighbouring regions of Durham and Cumbria. The control schools were selected in a similar manner to intervention schools, whereby schools were invited to participate in the evaluation but not receive the intervention (34 schools). Thirteen schools expressed an interest. After analysing academic achievement and demographic profiles for these 13 schools, a sub-sample of four schools was identified as having levels of academic achievement and demographic composition within the same range as the six intervention schools. These four control schools, two from Cumbria and two from Durham, were therefore chosen for inclusion in the outcome study.

Administration Procedure

Pupils completed the questionnaire in confidential conditions, in a venue such as the school assembly hall. Professional market research interviewers were present to introduce the survey, provide guidance and supervise completion and collection. Respondents were not required to write their name on the questionnaire and were given an envelope in which to seal their questionnaire before returning it directly to the interviewers present.

To allow the evaluation to continue beyond school leaving age, pupils were asked to complete a consent form asking them to indicate their willingness (or otherwise) to participate in a follow-up survey by post, and to provide their name and address for the mailing process. A postal survey was conducted in Autumn 1999. To encourage response, all respondents completing and returning a survey were sent a £10 gift voucher.

Measures

Primary outcome measures collected included: ever and recent experimentation with drugs; age of first experimentation; frequency of drug taking; and whether drugs were taken in combination with other drugs and/or alcohol.

Secondary outcome measures included: the number of drugs taken; experience of perceived harmful effects from drugs and parental communication about drugs.

In addition, data were collected concerning tobacco and alcohol use, perceived harm from drugs, future intentions about drug use, and experiences of education about drugs. The questionnaire was designed to test consistency of responses with regard to drug use and thus maximise validity of the data. Prior to the baseline survey the questionnaire was piloted using qualitative and quantitative methods. More information on the pilot is contained in the previous DPAS paper. The questionnaires are available upon request to the authors.

Response Rate and Sample Profile

At baseline a total of 1,984 questionnaires were completed. After thorough checking and coding of questionnaires had been conducted, 48 questionnaires (equivalent to 2%) were excluded from the analysis as they contained inconsistent or dubious responses. Questionnaires containing inconsistent or dubious responses were also excluded from subsequent follow-up surveys.

At the first follow-up a total of 1,883 questionnaires were completed and 132 (equivalent to 7%) were excluded. A total of 1,705 questionnaires were completed at the second follow-up and 126 (7%) were excluded. At the third follow-up a total of 1,447 questionnaires were completed and 18 (1%) were excluded.

Table 2.2 indicates an overall valid response rate of 87% at baseline, 79% at the first follow-up, 71% at the second follow-up and 64% at the third follow-up. At the second follow-up the response rate at one school (School 9) was particularly low, with only 27% participating. The day on which the survey administration took place coincided with exam and study leave. As a result only a small number of pupils were available to participate. Attempts were made to arrange a further date on which to repeat the survey but the school felt that no further time could be spared.

Table 2.3 details the profile of the sample. At baseline there were equal proportions of males and females in the sample. The first follow-up and the second follow-up surveys report only 43% males, with 4% and 5% respectively 'not stated'. It may be that males were more reluctant to complete the section on personal details and that these 'not stated' responses comprised mainly males. The distribution of parental employment and car ownership appears to be similar at each survey stage. Therefore, despite the exclusion of some questionnaires at each stage, the characteristics of each sample appear similar.

Analysis

The level of successful matching of individual respondents between the baseline and follow-up surveys was low, due to respondents' reluctance to disclose identifying information. As a result of this low level of matching, it was necessary to employ two strategies for analysis:

- providing confidence intervals (upper and lower limits for estimated prevalence) for non-independent samples of cross-sectional data at baseline, and each follow-up.

- statistical significance tests on variance in drug experiences by intervention level, to provide information against outcome measures, focused on matched data.

Table 2.2: Response Rate By School

| | Approximate Year 9/Year 10 size | Baseline | | 1st Follow-up | | 2nd Follow-up | | 3rd Follow-up | |
		Achieved sample	Approximate response rate	Achieved sample	Approximate response rate	Achieved sample	Approximate response rate	Achieved sample	Approximate response rate
School									
1	200	174	87%	163	82%	169	85%	146	73%
2	220	186	85%	175	80%	173	77%	140	64%
3	213	165	77%	168	79%	182	85%	141	66%
4	220	197	90%	160	73%	151	69%	141	64%
5	225	195	87%	183	81%	173	77%	153	68%
6	215	190	88%	173	80%	165	77%	166	77%
7	180	159	88%	146	81%	138	77%	100	56%
8	180	162	90%	141	78%	130	72%	99	55%
9	275	254	92%	218	79%	75	27%	163	59%
10	300	254	85%	224	75%	223	74%	180	60%
	2228	1936	87%	1751	79%	1579	71%	1429	64%

Table 2.3: Sample Profile

	Baseline		1st Follow-up		2nd Follow-up		3rd Follow-up	
	Actual Number	%	Actual Number	%	Actual Number	%	Actual Number	%
Gender								
Male	941	49	756	43	679	43	648	45
Female	964	50	926	53	816	52	781	55
Not stated	31	2	69	4	84	5	–	–
	1936	100	1751	100	1579	100	1429	100
Intervention Level								
Full	525	27	506	29	524	33	427	30
Partial	582	30	516	29	489	31	460	32
Control	829	43	729	42	566	36	542	38
	1936	100	1751	100	1579	100	1429	100
Parental Employment								
Both full-time	692	36	652	37	600	38	560	39
One full-time and one part-time	498	26	496	28	426	27	421	29
Both part-time or one full-time	343	18	303	17	280	18	242	17
One part-time	77	4	85	5	62	4	70	5
Neither working	140	7	103	6	106	7	90	6
Not stated	186	10	112	6	105	7	46	3
	1936	100	1751	100	1579	100	1429	100
Car Ownership								
No	248	13	229	13	198	13	153	11
Yes, one	1015	52	833	48	703	45	693	48
Yes, two or more	625	32	648	37	622	39	563	39
Not stated	48	2	41	2	56	4	20	1
	1936	100	1751	100	1579	100	1429	100

N.B. Due to rounding, percentages do not always add to 100%

2.2 PROCESS EVALUATION

Process evaluation concerns the means of implementing an intervention. It documents and describes three main aspects: what was delivered (dose), how it was delivered (integrity of delivery), and the target group's immediate response to what was delivered (response) (Flora et al 1993). Process evaluation also examines how effectively intervention partners collaborate, and the extent to which they have similar levels of understanding of and satisfaction with programme objectives (Fawcett et al 1997).

The process evaluation used a combination of qualitative research techniques and monitoring to examine the processes by which the intervention was delivered in each year. The aims were to:

- document and describe the programme and its implementation, and establish lessons learnt and their implications for good practice.

- offer guidance for refining the intervention stage under observation.

- provide an opportunity for secondary target groups to respond to proposals for future interventions.

Methods used included observation of workshops, focus groups with young people and parents, and individual in-depth interviews with teachers, actors and other agents of intervention delivery. More information on the process evaluation methodology is provided in the relevant reports (Stead et al 1997, Stead et al 1998, Jackson et al 2000).

2.3 IMPACT EVALUATION

The impact evaluation monitored the response of the primary target group to the Year Nine and Year Ten interventions in terms of a variety of measures including appreciation, participation and perceived efficacy. Methods were the same as for the outcome evaluation, but with the self-completion survey being administered two weeks after the intervention in the six intervention schools only. A total of 1,070 questionnaires were completed at Year Ten intervention schools, equivalent to an 80% response rate. A total of 35 questionnaires (equivalent to 3%) were excluded from the analysis as they contained inconsistent or dubious responses.

In order to develop and pilot the questionnaire, qualitative research, in the form of focus groups, was conducted with pupils from a selection of the schools, which were not involved in the evaluation but had received the intervention. This process ensured that the questionnaire included relevant measures that enabled the young people to effectively communicate their experiences and opinions of the intervention. More information on the measures taken in the Year Ten impact survey is provided in Chapter 4. Copies of the impact questionnaires are available upon request to the authors.

No impact survey was conducted following the Year Eleven intervention because: (a) it involved a smaller proportion of the cohort; and (b) the diverse range of intervention activities precluded the design of a standard questionnaire. Instead, response to the Year Eleven intervention was assessed at a process level, using qualitative methods such as focus groups, observation and individual in-depth interviews. More information is provided in Chapter 5.

2.4 FORMATIVE RESEARCH

Formative research was used to inform the development of the overall programme strategy, to assess needs and to refine specific intervention components (e.g. Coffield & Ridley 1992, Haywood et al 1993, Ridley 1995a and 1995b, Stead et al 1996). Methods used included:

- exploratory qualitative research with young people, parents, teachers, and the intervention partners.
- mapping exercises to profile the local communities around the three full intervention schools.
- secondary research examining the drugs prevention literature.
- concept testing of component options.
- pretesting of draft materials.

Formative research was conducted throughout programme implementation, to ensure that intervention design could accommodate changes in the needs of the target group and respond flexibly to emerging issues and priorities. Feedback from the formative research programme was provided quickly and on a continuous basis to the intervention team. In these ways, the formative research served an active research function (e.g. Allison & Rootman 1996) and was an integral element of programme implementation (Hastings et al 1997).

2.5 SUMMARY

NE Choices was evaluated at a number of levels. An outcome evaluation using a longitudinal quasi-experimental study examined whether or not the behavioural outcomes were met. This was conducted over four years with a cohort from six intervention and four control schools. Process evaluation assessed the implementation of the programme, examining what was delivered, how it was delivered, and responses and perceptions among target groups and intervention partners. Impact evaluation monitored the primary target group's response in terms of a variety of measures. Finally, a flexible and responsive programme of formative research informed the design and delivery of intervention components throughout.

3. IMPLEMENTING THE YEAR TEN AND ELEVEN INTERVENTIONS

This section describes the development and implementation of the Year Ten and Eleven interventions. The first section discusses the development of the two interventions, which began immediately after delivery of the Year Nine intervention in April 1997. The second section outlines the implementation of the Year Ten intervention, which took place between January and April 1998, and of the Year Eleven intervention, which was delivered between August 1998 and March 1999.

3.1 DEVELOPMENT OF THE YEAR TEN AND ELEVEN INTERVENTIONS

Findings from the process evaluation and impact survey for the Year Nine intervention were used to guide the content of the next two years of intervention. A number of specific recommendations emerged from these research exercises:

(i)   Drama should continue to be used as a programme medium

The research indicated that drama appeared to be an effective medium for engaging young people and stimulating discussion and reflection on drug use. However, it was felt that any new drama components should, firstly, be innovative to maintain the target's interest, and secondly, reflect the target's greater maturity and increasing exposure to drugs and drug use. It was therefore decided that the core component in the Year Ten intervention would be an out-of-school day-long drama and multi-media workshop in which young people would play a much more active role. The story, characters, themes and information content would have a greater emphasis on harm reduction than in Year Nine, to reflect changing drug use patterns (Home Office Drugs Prevention Initiative 1998).

(ii)   Information products and media activity should continue to form part of the programme

Positive responses to the Year Nine NE Choices Magazine and Family Fact File confirmed an ongoing need for credible and attractive information products for young people and parents. It was decided that a new product would be developed for young people to reflect their changing tastes, and that a range of products in other media would be researched. Because the Year Nine promotional activity and press publicity were felt to have been slightly weak elements, it was also decided that these elements of the programme should be enhanced in Years Ten and Eleven.

(iii)   Classroom follow-up work should be more intensive and better supported

The classroom follow-up component in the Year Nine intervention had been patchily delivered, and inadequately supported. It was therefore decided to intensify this component by requiring participating schools to make a formal commitment that all Year Ten pupils would receive a standard amount of follow-up, organised within each school to suit its own PSHE curriculum. To support and facilitate this, NDPT would provide tailored training to all teachers involved, and provide supply cover funding to enable teachers to attend the training. This would be reinforced by a more substantial and tailored pack of resource materials (Home Office Drugs Prevention Initiative 1998).

(iv)   Parents would continue to be supported

The Year Nine intervention evaluation suggested that parents were a difficult group to recruit into drugs prevention programmes, and that there was limited demand even among the more motivated parents for more intensive support. However, parents did feel in need of ongoing information, and welcomed the opening of a channel of communication between them and the schools on the subject of drugs. It was therefore decided that parents would continue to be supported in two ways. Firstly, an intervention focusing on parent-child communication about drugs would be offered to all Year Eleven parents. Secondly, a worker would be employed to build links with parents through outreach work and to offer drugs awareness sessions and support as needed (Home Office Drugs Prevention Initiative 1998).

(v)   The programme would gradually move into other settings

Research into young people's receptiveness to health education interventions suggests that there is an increasing disaffection with school as they grow older (Nutbeam & Aaro 1991, Nutbeam et al 1993b). It was decided that the Year Eleven intervention would be delivered largely through non-school settings, such as youth work and outreach, to maintain interest and appeal for this age group (Home Office Drugs Prevention Initiative 1998). This decision was further supported by comments from teachers that there was little room in the Year Eleven curriculum for intensive drugs education work.

(vi)   High-risk groups would be targeted

Finally, it was decided that increased segmentation and targeting would be valuable, particularly to address the needs of 'high risk' young people, whose specific needs could not be met fully in a whole-population intervention. A component specifically for high-risk young people was therefore developed for implementation as part of the Year Eleven intervention.

In addition to these recommendations from the Year Nine intervention, additional formative research was conducted to provide guidance on specific intervention questions. This included literature reviews into the value of interactive methods, drama-based approaches and peer work, and into specific approaches targeting the 14-16 age group; a mapping of community profiles and networking around the full intervention schools to explore the most appropriate channels for reaching secondary school parents; and focus group research with parents to explore interest in and demand for parent-targeted information and support.

In June 1997 NDPT convened an expert panel that was charged with the task of synthesising information from the various research exercises and producing recommendations for the concepts underpinning the Year Ten and Eleven interventions. The panel comprised members of NDPT, the Drugs Prevention Initiative (DPI), local authorities, teachers, Northern Stage, Procter & Gamble, drugs prevention consultants and the evaluation team.

The panel's recommendations were translated into an outline strategy and operationalised. The timescale was extremely tight: while the Year Nine intervention had been developed and piloted over 18 months, only six months were available to develop and refine the Year Ten intervention. This put a great deal of strain on the intervention partners. A Creative Director was appointed in November to work with Northern Stage theatre company to develop an outline script for the drama component, appoint actors, and oversee the selection and design of the venue. The first task of the Creative Director was to devise the format of the out-of-school drama and multi-media workshop, which is outlined in Figure 3.1.

Figure 3.1: Outline of Year Ten Intervention Drama Workshop

Pupils worked in self-selecting peer groups of around ten to investigate the disappearance of a fictional 17-year old girl, Rachel (who appeared only on a pre-recorded video clip). To fulfil the quest the peer groups visited a series of seven rooms, five of which contained a fictional character who had some involvement with Rachel (e.g. Mam, friend etc.) and represented a different view of drugs. The characters performed a short piece of drama then answered questions put by the groups of pupils. The 'Secrets and Lies' room contained multi-media materials designed to explore facts and opinions regarding drugs.

Groups also had the use of a computer with interactive software, which contained further information about the characters, and took part in drugs education activities facilitated by the actors. One task involved producing a newspaper article about Rachel's disappearance. The diagram depicts the workshop visually.

Rooms were decorated to match character (e.g. Mam had a sitting room, Darren an old allotment shed)

Large attic-type space painted black

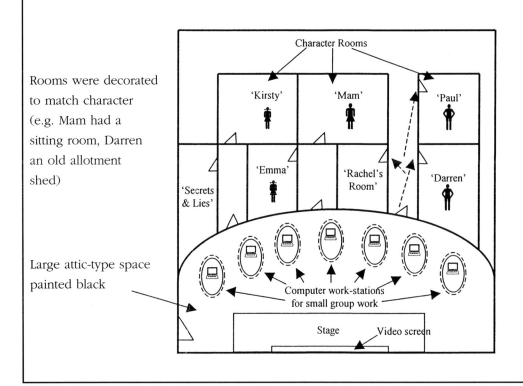

Following this devising period, auditions were held for the parts of the five characters in Rachel's life and two all-round facilitators. Seven actor-facilitators were appointed and contracted to work for a four-week rehearsal period beginning in December 1997 and three months of delivery between January and April 1998.

3. IMPLEMENTING THE YEAR TEN AND ELEVEN INTERVENTIONS

A major challenge was locating a venue that was large, central, capable of being transformed into an exciting multi-media environment, available for exclusive use over the intervention period, and affordable. The top floor of the Discovery Museum in Newcastle City centre was selected. Tyne and Wear Museums Service donated this space free for three months. However, the space was not available until mid-January, which severely constrained the time available to build and install the sets and multi-media equipment (the first school was scheduled to visit at the end of January).

Around Christmas, a series of formative research and piloting exercises were conducted with groups of Year Ten pupils from non-intervention schools, to help develop the characters and storylines, and also to pilot the full workshop session. Findings from these exercises led to a number of improvements to the workshop, the most notable being an increase in the face-to-face facilitation provided. Further observations and focus groups were conducted during the first week of the formal delivery period to check whether any further changes were needed. Findings from these identified some weaknesses with the drugs education activities, which seemed less successful in engaging pupils compared with the drama elements of the day. A decision was taken to replace the drugs education activities with a piece of theatre which would elaborate on the themes raised in the visits to characters. However, this decision meant that the new element had to be developed while the intervention was being delivered; this had implications for the consistency of delivery (see Section 3.2 below).

Preparation of schools for the intervention began in September 1997. A one-day teacher-training course was delivered to all intervention school teachers responsible for Year Ten tutoring and guidance, and PSHE. The aim of the course was to equip teachers with the confidence, knowledge and skills to conduct a programme of classroom support and follow-up work to the core drama component. A Teachers' Manual was developed to support this work. Both the manual and the training course were piloted. In addition, NDPT paid a briefing visit to each of the 13 schools participating in the Year Ten intervention to discuss the aim and nature of the drama component and to finalise details of each schools' visit to the Discovery Museum. A local bus company was contracted to provide a delivery service from school to museum, and was painted in NE Choices imagery and logos.

Multi-media elements to support the drama workshop were developed by Sunderland University. These included interactive computer software and video material. Media and information products were developed by NDPT and Procter & Gamble. The main media product for Year Ten pupils was the Factfile, a filofax-type product for use during the drama workshop and afterwards as a personal organiser. This was pretested with a group of Year Ten pupils. Other media products included the Teachers' Manual already mentioned, the Family Fact File and Governor Fact File developed for the Year Nine intervention, and promotional materials. NDPT also negotiated with the then Health Education Authority that each participating Year Ten pupil would receive free the HEA's CD-Rom 'D-Code'.

Development of the Year Eleven intervention began as the Year Ten intervention was being implemented. As outlined previously, it was decided that the main component of the Year Eleven intervention would use youth work methods, with a youth work project being loosely attached to each intervention school (13 in all) for six months, with NDPT funding for staff, resources and activities. All Year Ten pupils would be given the opportunity to volunteer for the projects, whose aim would be to develop skills to enable participants to devise and deliver a piece of drugs education work of their own choosing to their peers. The delivery to peers would mean that each project would have a potentially wider reach than simply the smaller number participating directly.

During the Year Ten intervention period, therefore, NDPT held meetings with managers of all the local statutory and voluntary sector youth services to explain the intervention aims and gauge the willingness and capacity of youth work services to respond. Enough interest was expressed that two youth workers could be found, from a mixture of statutory and voluntary services, for each of the thirteen proposed projects. NDPT agreed to pay half of the salary costs for each of the workers, with employers paying the remaining costs. Each youth worker was contracted to provide 30 sessions of work at three hours a session, with each group deciding how that time was allocated. In April 1998, a two-day training course was offered to the statutory and voluntary sector youth workers in post at the time. In addition to staff costs, NDPT also provided funding for each group to attend a residential session at which more intensive work could take place. Each youth group was given an operational budget of £1,000, and could bid for additional funding from a pool of £20,000 for specific training and activity work. Some local authorities also provided money; for example, Northumberland contributed £6,000 of 'Standards' money from the Department of Education, for which the two Northumberland LEA schools could apply.

The Year Eleven parents' programme was developed over the same period. Exploratory research was conducted by Procter & Gamble with groups of Year Eleven parents to identify and explore their drugs information and other needs. Findings from the research were used to inform the development of a drama session for parents focusing on the theme of parent-child communication about drugs, and also of accompanying information materials (see 3.2 for more information). Finally, the Year Eleven programme for 'high risk' young people was also developed during the Year Ten intervention period. This was designed and delivered by Fairbridge Tyne and Wear, a charitable UK-wide organisation that works with young people who have social, behavioural and other difficulties. Its aims are to build confidence and skills, and to increase personal effectiveness and participation in society. Fairbridge's methods include outreach work, group work, outdoor activities, creative skills, training in job-related skills, and individual counselling and advice. NDPT contracted with Fairbridge to adapt its basic week-long course to meet the needs of a group of Year Eleven pupils and to incorporate a drugs prevention element in line with the aims and methods of NE Choices. It was also agreed that follow-up work would be conducted with course participants. NDPT made funding available to Fairbridge to run up to three courses, for a maximum of 36 young people. In September 1998, each of the six intervention evaluation schools was invited to identify up to six students who could potentially benefit from participation.

3.2 IMPLEMENTATION OF THE YEAR TEN AND ELEVEN INTERVENTIONS

The Year Ten and Eleven interventions were implemented in all six of the schools included in the three-year evaluation ('evaluation schools'), plus an additional seven schools for which DPAS provided funding. As described in Chapter 2, the six evaluation schools were divided between three receiving a full version of the intervention ('full intervention schools') and three receiving a partial version ('partial intervention schools'). The full intervention comprised all the intervention components, while the partial intervention comprised only those components aimed at the primary target group of young people.

In Years Ten and Eleven, the difference between partial and full schools was less pronounced than in Year Nine, the main contrast being that partial intervention schools were not offered the Year Eleven drugs awareness sessions for parents. However, as these reached a relatively small number of parents, this distinction is unlikely to have had a significant impact. In other respects the full and partial schools received a similar range of components.

Implementation was examined in all six of the evaluation schools. Two research exercises provided information on implementation: the process evaluation, which used observation, individual in-depth interview and focus group methods; and the 1998 impact survey, a self-completion questionnaire administered to all Year Ten pupils in the evaluation schools (see Chapter 2 for more details).

This section focuses on delivery in the six evaluation schools, although some information is provided on delivery in all 13 of the participating schools where this is available.

Year Ten out-of-school Drama Workshop

Forty-six one-day out-of-school drama workshops were delivered to Year Ten pupils in the 13 participating schools. Each school sent pupils to the museum over three to four days, with groups of between 28 and 90 attending each day. In terms of reach, the workshop was attended by the vast majority of the optimum target of 3,050 (the full Year Ten intake in the 13 schools). Impact survey data indicate that 94% of Year Ten pupils reported having attended. Attendance might have been negatively affected by the requirement that pupils obtain parental permission (because the workshop was held out of school), which some forgot to do. Encouragingly, however, teachers noted in interview that ordinary absenteeism levels appeared to be lower than usual on the workshop days, suggesting that poorly attending pupils made an effort to attend on the day of the intervention.

As noted above, the drama workshop was modified in content during the intervention period. This had implications for delivery consistency. The first three schools received the original version of the workshop, comprising the themed quest and visits to character rooms in the morning and drugs education activities, including producing a newspaper article, in the afternoon. At this stage, the decision was taken to replace the drugs education activities with a piece of theatre. While this new element was being devised, the next two schools visiting the museum took part in a version of the workshop, which contained only the themed quest and visits to characters rooms and the newspaper article task. The final eight schools received the final version, comprising themed quest, visits to rooms and the live theatre. Of the six evaluation schools, two received the second version and four the third version.

The actors felt that the variations in pupil numbers could have affected the quality of pupils' experience of the workshop: where numbers exceeded 80, groups appeared to engage less intensively with the workshop, while groups that were too small (under 40) lacked energy. Responsibility for pupil numbers was attributed to schools, who, despite detailed briefing on the workshop by NDPT, did not always adhere to the recommended number of 60 pupils per day. The presence of teachers at the workshop was felt to be largely unproblematic, although on two occasions accompanying teachers intervened to discipline pupils in ways which the actors felt were heavy handed and potentially disruptive to their own rapport with pupils. A final minor difficulty with delivery was the occasional unreliability of the NE Choices bus, which once or twice failed to collect pupils from the museum.

Overall, however, delivery of the drama workshop appeared to have been consistent with programme objectives. The small group work and interactive tasks appeared to generate more active participation than the Year Nine drama workshop had done. The drugs messages communicated by the actors were consistent with NE Choices themes, and placed a greater emphasis than the Year Nine workshop on harm reduction and also on heroin, which local drugs prevention experts believed was becoming more prevalent in the north-east at the time. The themes of choices and consequences were stressed by placing drugs use in the context of other adolescent choices regarding, for example, alcohol, smoking, sexuality, education, and careers.

The Year Ten and Year Nine drama workshops were different in several respects. The Year Ten workshop was more challenging to deliver; involved more actors, a large and complex venue, and was more sustained and intensive in its performance. However, the use of one central venue allowed greater control over delivery than had been possible in Year Nine, when the drama team had had to adapt to different school environments and procedures every week. The Year Ten actors felt that the greater consistency in delivery was reflected in the response of pupils, which displayed fewer differences by school. Against this greater consistency in overall delivery was a greater degree of variety *within* each overall school group in the ways the small self-selected peer groups engaged with the workshop. These variations reflected their different peer dynamics and attitudes to drugs, and resulted in a more diverse and personal learning experience, as had been hoped. It was anticipated the Year Eleven youth work intervention would take this diversification further.

Year Ten Classroom Follow-up

Participating schools had been briefed to deliver four classroom sessions to follow-up the drama session at the museum. The teacher training course and Teachers' Manual had provided lesson plans and worksheets, although teachers were encouraged to adapt these to suit their varying curricula and methods. In practice, schools delivered varying amounts of follow-up. In the six evaluation schools, follow-up ranged from a brief discussion in one school to eight hours in another. On average, schools delivered around one to two sessions, or two hours. Impact survey data indicated that the proportion of pupils recalling any classroom follow-up ranged from 8% in the school that delivered least to 69% in the school which delivered most. Follow-up sessions were structured into the curriculum in different ways. For example, in one school follow-up was incorporated into the weekly 40-minute tutorial programme and delivered by all 12 Year Ten tutors. In another school, follow-up was delivered in the specialist PHSE programme taught by two specialist PSE teachers. Two schools delivered some follow-up in RE lessons. There were also differences in the degree of in-school co-ordination, with, for example, teachers in one school agreeing a standard four-session outline for the follow-up, and teachers in another school adopting a more discretionary individual approach.

Within schools, there were variations between individual teachers. Some were more comfortable with harm reduction messages than others, and a few favoured a more prescriptive approach to drugs than that associated with NE Choices. Nevertheless, the Year Ten follow-up represented an improvement on that delivered in Year Nine, being both more sustained and having a greater, although sub-optimal, degree of consistency. Overall, the evaluation of this element of the intervention suggests that there may be limits to the consistency that can be achieved in schools, even where a programme is supported by standardised materials and training and by a robust and highly consistent core component (the drama workshop).

Year Eleven Youth-led Projects

Youth work projects were implemented in all 13 participating schools. In summary, each project comprised a group of between 4 and 10 young people which met for six months to participate in drugs-related youth work and to develop a drugs education 'product' for delivery to the young people's peers. Within the six evaluation schools, all six projects produced such a product, including a display, drama workshops, games and a video. Five were delivered to (ie. shown to or performed with) other groups of young people. Figure 3.2 presents a summary of these six projects.

Figure 3.2: Outline of Youth-led Projects in the Six Evaluation Schools

Project	Project description	Project workers	Project participants	Project activities	Delivery of 'product'
1	Interactive display ("The Wall") comprising five six-foot high cabinets each containing a type of drug and drug dealer. Cabinets could be covered by bricks, representing knowledge about drugs.	One male worker, employed by Local Authority (LA). One female worker, p/t co-worker, funded by NDPT. Additional input by video worker.	Large group at start, changed substantially over intervention period. Final group comprised five males and five females.	25 weekly two-hour sessions. Initial sessions on increasing drugs knowledge. Early ideas to develop a video were dropped. Residential (four days) at outdoor activity centre.	"The Wall" installed in school canteen for five days. All 200 Year Eleven pupils viewed "The Wall" and completed questionnaires, plus 500 pupils from other year groups.
2	Video board game. Players move round a board by watching video clips depicting different drug scenarios and answering questions based on the scenarios.	One female worker, employed by voluntary sector. One male p/t co-worker, funded by NDPT. Additional input by community artist.	Initial group of 12. Males dropped out leaving final group of seven females.	25 weekly three-hour sessions. Outdoor activities. Three-day residential.	Game played (but not completed) with two Year Nine classes. Attempted to negotiate session with Year Eleven classes, but permission refused.
3	Drama workshop, comprising a play about girl taking ecstasy at a party, followed by interactive quiz and discussion.	One female worker, employed by voluntary sector. One female co-ordinator, funded by NDPT. Input from drama worker.	Following high demand, group reduced to six, then four females.	26 weekly three-hour sessions. Attended another drama project for ideas. Residential weekend involving teamwork and outdoor activities.	Workshop performed for two groups of Year Seven pupils in own school and two groups of Year Eleven pupils from neighbouring schools.
4	Video featuring Jerry Springer-type talk show. Participants played the parts of host and three drug-taking guests.	One male worker, employed by LA. One female co-worker, funded by NDPT. Input from 'Black Box', a video company.	Began with two groups of 10 each, one largely male and one largely female. Merger of groups resulting in several females dropping out. Final group of three females and six males.	Weekly two-hour sessions. Residential weekend included outdoor activities and video training. Video shooting took place over last two months.	Video not completed by end of intervention period. Group hoped to show video to Year Ten and Eleven pupils in neighbouring school.
5	Drama workshop, comprising a play about 'good' and 'bad' twins faced with drug choices, and an interactive quiz.	One female worker employed by LA. Support from youth workers at neighbouring school. Input from drama worker.	Eight females.	31 weekly two-hour sessions. Residential weekend with participants from a neighbouring school. Drama training provided 4 months into project.	Performed to a group of 10-11 year olds at local youth club, to 60 Year Nine pupils at participants' own school, and to 30 Year Eleven pupils at neighbouring schools.
6	Floor game based on 'Twister'. Players moved forward by answering questions about different drugs and forfeits were performed for wrong answers.	One male worker, employed by LA. One female p/t co-worker, funded by NDPT. Input from community artists.	Two females and four males.	Approximately 17 weekly two-hour sessions. Early phase of project was disrupted by changes in school personnel, resulting in a two-month delay. Residential period spent on artwork.	Game played with members of local youth club, and with younger pupils at participants' school. No plans were made to use game with Year Elevens.

Recruitment of project participants began at the Year Ten intervention drama workshop, at Newcastle's Discovery Museum (see Section 3.2 above). The actors concluded each daily workshop by describing the forthcoming projects and presenting them as an opportunity to do further drama or artwork as part of NE Choices. They invited those pupils who were interested to leave their names and addresses so that they could be contacted over the summer holiday. NDPT had decided that the drama workshop represented an ideal recruitment opportunity for the youth work projects because of the potential to capitalise on the enthusiasm and interest generated by the day. This largely proved to be the case, with each daily workshop yielding between a dozen and 80 names, resulting in up to 100 potential participants from some schools. The challenge then was to reduce numbers to sizes that would be conducive to intensive group work. Some youth workers initially invited all interested young people to a briefing or taster day in order to filter out the less interested. In some cases, youth workers deliberately stressed some of the more 'negative' aspects of the projects (such as the regular commitment to meet) in order to reduce numbers. This process was largely successful. However, in one project the school intervened in the recruitment process, pushing the youth workers to select more academic and motivated pupils. Although the youth workers argued that the project might be of more benefit to the less academically able and more 'problematic' pupils, the school's preference prevailed. For two of the schools, initial recruitment through the Year Ten drama workshop either yielded too few numbers or did not take place at all because of time constraints. In these cases, the youth workers had to use alternative, more time-consuming methods to generate names (e.g. visits to school assembly), before they could begin the filtering process.

It had been expected that each project would deliver its 'product' to participants' peer group of Year Eleven pupils. However, some participants were reluctant to perform to or work with their peers. Three projects consequently delivered their project to Year Elevens in neighbouring schools, rather than their own; four delivered instead or as well to younger age groups, ranging from Year Seven to Year Nine. One project, the video by School Four, was not completed by the end of the evaluation period. The project by School One ("The Wall") had the greatest reach, being shown to all Year Eleven pupils in participants' own school and around 500 pupils from other year groups in the school. In total, around 340 Year Eleven pupils were involved, either as project participants or recipients, plus around 700 younger pupils.

Video Box

The project work was complemented by the Video Box, a walk-in interactive installation featuring a compilation of project work from the intervention schools. The core aim was to collate material in a manner that was engaging, cohesive and able to serve as a method of widening the projects' reach.

The Box was designed as a self-contained mobile multi-media exhibition space capable of accommodating a full class of pupils. Youth-led project material from schools was edited into an 18-minute video that was presented via television screens and speakers inside the box. Static images were magnified and mounted onto the interior walls, and above each, a 'fact card' displayed key drugs information developed by the youth-led groups.

The Video Box completed a five-week tour covering eight schools. Five of these were intervention evaluation schools, and three were non-evaluation schools. Within each school, the Video Box could be accessed in two ways:

1. Facilitated timetabled sessions, in which class groups attended the Box during lesson time.
2. Stand alone device available at break times and lunch times for unfacilitated visits.

Approximately 785 Year Eleven pupils experienced the Video Box within a facilitated session. In addition, around 168 Year Tens took part in a facilitated session, and it was estimated that a further 140 pupils interacted with the Box in its stand-alone version. Overall, the Video Box reached approximately 1,093 young people across the eight schools, nearly four-fifths of whom were in the Year Eleven target group.

Facilitated Timetabled Sessions

The duration of timetabled sessions varied from 30 to 80 minutes. When timetabling allowed, the sessions followed a standard format. Two facilitators, one male and one female, conducted the session. The class group was brought to the space outside the Box, which had seating arranged. One facilitator provided a brief introduction to the content and history of the Box, and then took the young people inside to watch the 18-minute video. 'Post-video exercises' were then conducted outside the Box. Seven cards had been pinned onto the exterior walls of the box while the pupils were inside, six of which represented more detailed information on the video box 'fact cards' positioned inside. The seventh card was blank.

The class was divided into smaller groups, which were asked to rank the cards in order of importance. They were then asked to identify missing pieces of information or gaps in the issues covered by the fact cards and the video. These were written on the blank cards. At the end of each session, the groups presented their results to the rest of the class and small group discussions analysed the session.

Most of the longer sessions successfully followed this format. However, in the shorter sessions the facilitators struggled to cover all the material, and in the shortest two sessions the post-video workshop had to be excluded. In larger classes, young people aided facilitation of the session.

Stand Alone Device

Two of the eight schools made the Video Box available on a stand-alone basis. Invitation cards were circulated to pupils, advertising the Video Box and encouraging pupils to view the box. The video was on a loop recording and ran for a full break period. The Video Box appeared to have aroused a reasonable level of curiosity, and reached a wider age range than the classroom sessions.

Response to Video Box

Feedback questionnaires to 470 young people in four of the eight schools recorded the reaction to the Video Box. The following results were obtained.

- Eighteen percent found the **Video Box** to be 'dull', 50% found it 'OK', and 32% found it 'interesting'.

- Sixteen percent found the **workshop** 'dull', 52% found it 'OK', and 32% found it 'interesting'.

- Twenty one percent thought that the **drugs information** did 'tell me new stuff', 57% thought it did 'remind me of stuff I knew before', and 22% thought it 'told me things I knew'.

- Eighty-two percent of young people felt that drugs information was more interesting if created by young people for young people.

In addition, the questionnaire asked: 'What is the one thing you've learnt / will remember from Video Box or the workshop?'. The majority of young people commented on the different messages they received surrounding the dangers of drug use and harm reduction methods:

"Drugs can never be safe, but you can make the environment in which taking them safer."
"Don't inject drugs."
"That street drugs are cut."
"The effects of mixing drugs."

(Year Elevens)

The two facilitators also provided some feedback on the sessions. The key points that arose were:

- Prior preparation in the schools appeared to have varied widely, with some schools appearing to have planned carefully for the Box's arrival and stay, and others appearing to have given it little thought.

- Facilitation of the workshop session was made more difficult by the varying lengths of time allowed by the school timetable.

- The level of drugs knowledge among pupils visiting the Box varied widely within and between schools. This suggested that, like previous NE Choices components, the Box reached young people with a wide range of drug attitudes and experiences.

- Levels of engagement in the session varied widely between different class groups. Some of these differences were attributed to the physical environment and timetabling, others to the composition of the groups.

- The classroom sessions were improved upon over time, in terms of delivery and organisation, as the facilitators became more experienced.

- The stand-alone format was perceived as less effective than the facilitated session as it failed to contextualise the Box and to encourage discussion and learning.

In conclusion, it was felt that although Video Box was well received by many young people, it did not present the youth-led work in an optimal way. There were concerns about the sound quality, which was seen to have been hindered by a low budget and little development time.

Year Eleven Parents' Drama-based Drug Awareness Sessions

Six drug awareness sessions for parents were delivered, two for each of the three 'full intervention' evaluation schools. One of each pair of sessions was held in the school, while the other was held in a community venue. The sessions were structured around an interactive drama performance about the drugs and alcohol choices facing a group of 16-17 year olds, and about parent-child communication about drugs. Actor-facilitators intercepted each scenario at strategic points and invited the audience to suggest alternative ways in which the young people could respond to the challenges and pressures depicted. The actors took on board the advice of audience members and re-enacted the scenes incorporating the parents' suggestions. A circular blackboard was placed on the floor in the centre of the performance arena, on which the actor-facilitators wrote key issues and messages raised by the audience. Parents were invited to examine the blackboard after the drama session. Each session ran for one hour and 45 minutes on average.

Three of the sessions were observed for the evaluation. Audience size varied greatly within the three sessions observed, ranging from two to 20 parents. Sessions held in the schools tended to be slightly better attended than sessions held in other venues. Low audience numbers did not appear to have too detrimental an effect on the session, with parents at poorly attended workshops appearing enthusiastic, interested and willing to interact throughout.

There was a high degree of consistency between sessions in overall structure and length. In terms of approach, tone and key messages, the parents drug workshops were consistent with NDPT's expectations and the objectives of NE Choices. The session incorporated some harm reduction themes, although it tended to focus more on the range of choices young people face regarding experimentation with drugs, alcohol consumption, friendship groups, peer pressure, relationships with parents, and deception. It also touched on the social consequences of addiction.

Parents' Support Groups

A community worker was contacted by NDPT to work on an outreach basis with groups of parents interested in learning more about drugs within an informal setting. Contact was made through existing networks that were both formal (e.g. tenants' associations, community centres) and informal (e.g. word of mouth, friends). Twelve group sessions were conducted, in a mixture of private homes and community centres. Most of the interest came from parents in the communities surrounding the three full intervention schools, where the worker concentrated her efforts.

Year Eleven 'High Risk' Young People's Programme

A week-long course for 'high-risk' young people took place in December 1998/99. Although funding had been provided for up to 36 young people, the six schools identified a total of only 13 young people. This was despite prior suggestions from the schools that they welcomed the intervention and could readily identify sufficient pupils who could benefit. Neither Fairbridge nor the research team could establish why schools did not identify more pupils. A course was also conducted with a school not participating in the NE Choices evaluation. Funding for this was provided separately.

Schools were invited by NDPT to identify pupils who could be considered to be at high risk of engaging in drug use on the basis of meeting at least two of the following criteria: a history of truanting; lack of engagement with school; being at risk of or currently excluded from school; a history of behavioural problems; an involvement with social services, or an involvement with the youth justice system. Senior management in the schools were asked to work with Education Welfare Officers to identify and approach such pupils to explain the aim of the Fairbridge course and to arrange for Fairbridge staff to subsequently contact them directly. The extent to which schools used these selection criteria and followed the selection process suggested by NDPT is not known, although anecdotal evidence suggests that there was some variance between the schools in their method of selecting young people.

The 13 selected pupils were contacted by the Fairbridge outreach worker by telephone or letter and invited to a meeting in a local venue such as a cafe for an informal chat about Fairbridge and the course. This was quite a lengthy process that had to be handled sensitively. Eight of the 13 young people subsequently attended an open day at the Fairbridge base, which was used to familiarise the young people with Fairbridge staff, brief them on the aims and nature of the course, and assess the young people's circumstances and needs.

The course comprised a mixture of outdoor and indoor activities, group work and team building exercises, facilitated discussion, and unstructured relaxation time during which workers and participants chatted over coffee. Although the workers had an initial tentative structure for the course, this was frequently revised to reflect group interests and needs and other factors, such as the weather. Some activities took place on site at the Fairbridge base, while others required a mini-bus journey to an outdoor location. Activities included abseiling, a trust-building exercise, and a drugs discussion session. This was facilitated by a former drug addict working with Fairbridge. In the first part of the session, the facilitator talked about different types of drugs and their effects, while the second half of the session was more interactive, comprising a discussion in which young people shared their own experiences. The session was concluded by the Fairbridge team leader who made clear and overt references to NE Choices themes and messages. In addition to this overt drugs education input, Fairbridge workers also took informal opportunities to discuss drugs with the participants throughout the week.

A one-day follow-up session was conducted after the course. Participants shared their opinions on the most and least enjoyable parts of the course, the activities that had caused them most anxiety, and the achievements of which they were most proud. Inputs from the workers stressed themes of confidence, self-image and not being constrained by others' perceptions and expectations.

Longer-term follow-up was conducted by a female worker not involved in the original course. Participants were invited to a 'reunion' course involving more outdoor activities, following which they engaged in one-to-one follow-up and support to varying degrees.

Other Intervention Components

A number of other components were implemented over the Year Ten and Eleven intervention period. These included:

- Seventy-nine out of a total of 84 Year Ten and PSHE teachers attended a one-day teacher training course on how to conduct classroom follow-up to the drama workshop.

- All Year Ten pupils who attended the drama workshop received a Factfile specially designed to accompany the workshop, and a copy of a Health Development Agency (formerly Health Education Authority) CD-Rom 'D-Code'. The latter was provided free by the HDA. Pupils were also given CD-Roms of the NE Choices website and the website developed for the drama session at the Discovery Museum.

- Approximately 1,000 Family Fact Files (FFF) were distributed on request to Year Ten pupils from the 13 intervention schools during the year. (In Year Nine, 14,000 FFFs were distributed, bringing the total number of distributed files to 15,000.)

- Around 100 Governor Fact Files were distributed during the intervention period to governors in the 13 intervention schools.

- A press launch was held on 5th February 1998, and followed-up by weekly or fortnightly releases relating to aspects of NE Choices. Public relations and press work was contracted to a PR agency, Batwatch, following the recommendation from the Year Nine evaluation that more resources should be put into media work to increase community awareness of and support for NE Choices. The coverage achieved by the PR and press work comprised, on average, weekly news items in regional and local press, TV coverage of the Year Ten drama workshop launch and launch of the Year Eleven website, and TV coverage of two of the youth work projects. There was also radio coverage of the parents workshops in two schools, and of the Year Eleven website.

A table outlining all the intervention components over the three years of NE Choices is provided in Chapter 1 (see Figure 1.2).

3.3 Summary

The main components of the Year Ten intervention were delivered as planned and attained a high reach. The ambitious nature of the out-of-school multi-media drama workshop posed organisational and resource challenges, but yielded benefits in terms of greater control over delivery consistency. Classroom follow-up was more intensive and co-ordinated than in Year Nine, reflecting a greater input from NDPT in the form of a training programme and Teachers' Manual. Nevertheless, there were still substantial variations between schools, and between teachers within schools, in the amount and type of follow-up, suggesting that there are limits to the consistency of school intervention delivery which can be achieved, even when interventions are supported by standard training and materials.

The Year Eleven intervention, like the previous two intervention years, comprised a mix of interpersonal and media components and was delivered to both primary and secondary target groups. However, a substantial difference between the Year Eleven and previous years' interventions was in the design of the core interpersonal component for the primary target of Year Eleven pupils. The Year Eleven interpersonal component took the form of individual youth-led projects, each of which was unique, rather than being a standard package as in Years Nine and Ten. A far smaller number of pupils were involved – a self-selecting group of young people who volunteered to participate in their own time, rather than the whole population of Year Elevens. In addition, youth work, rather than the schools, was the major delivery channel. This decision was made because it was believed that by age 15 to 16, pupils would be less receptive to drugs education within the formal setting of school, and more receptive to input provided by an external source.

The different format of the core component had several implications. Firstly, the intervention messages, themes, and methods were more diverse than in previous years. It had been assumed that each youth group would choose to develop a project that was consistent with its own level of interest and experiences of drugs. For example, those with less experience of drugs might choose to concentrate on awareness raising, while those with more experience might choose to focus on risks and harm reduction. The diverse nature of the resulting projects appears to have borne this out. Secondly, the reach for the youth-led project intervention was much smaller than that of the Year Nine and Ten drama-based interventions, which targeted and largely reached the whole school year population. The Year Eleven youth-led project intervention directly involved 44 pupils from the six evaluation schools, and had a secondary audience of around 1,000 pupils in Years Seven to Eleven. However, the involvement of the project participants themselves was far more intense than in previous years: all groups met for several months, and the smaller size of the groups meant that participants' quality of interaction and learning was also greater. The reach of the Fairbridge intervention component was also smaller than the intended 36 young people, with only 13 potential participants being identified, and only eight taking part. Against this smaller reach must be balanced the potentially more intensive experience of participation and improved quality of learning. This is examined in Chapter 5.

4. REACTIONS OF YOUNG PEOPLE AND TEACHERS TO THE YEAR TEN INTERVENTION

The Year Ten intervention comprised an all-day out-of-school drama workshop, classroom support and follow-up, and a range of information products. The drama workshop, held in a specially designed multi-media set at the Discovery Museum, took the format of a themed quest (see Chapter 3 for more detailed information). This section examines the reactions of young people and teachers to elements of the Year Ten interventions, drawing on two sources:

- The process evaluation. This included observation of six drama workshops and three classroom follow-up sessions, eight focus groups with Year Ten pupils, and ten interviews with teaching staff in the six evaluation schools;

- The 1998 impact survey. This examined young people's participation, expectations, enjoyment, engagement and opinions in relation to elements of the intervention.

The impact survey, completed by 1,070 Year Ten pupils, examined young people's participation in and reactions to the drama workshop, their recall of classroom follow-up work, and their use of and reactions to some of the information products. There were two slightly different versions of the questionnaire to correspond with the different versions of the workshop (see Section 3.2). The main difference in the questionnaire was the inclusion of statements to assess response to the play performed in the afternoon in the later version of the workshop. Qualitative research was undertaken to develop and pilot the questionnaires.

The impact survey did not collect data on drug use as the main focus was on reaction to the intervention. As it was not possible to match all respondents to the earlier outcome survey the impact results cannot be analysed by drug use behaviour. However, data were collected on intentions to use drugs, a measure that correlates highly with previous drug use. Data in this chapter are analysed by gender and intention to take drugs. A range of statistical tests has been conducted to examine whether or not differences in response are likely to be due to chance. Where a difference is unlikely to be a spurious finding, a p-value is quoted that provides the likelihood of a difference as large as that observed being discovered by chance. Different thresholds for rejecting the role of chance are given, such as five per cent ($p<0.05$), one per cent ($p<0.01$) and so on. The smaller the figure the less likely it is that an observed difference is due to chance.

Section 4.1 discusses the reactions of young people to the drama workshop and Section 4.2 examines their reactions to the main information product, the Factfile. Both sections draw on findings from both the process evaluation and the impact survey. Section 4.3 examines the reactions of teachers to the intervention, drawing on findings from the process evaluation.

4.1 YOUNG PEOPLE'S REACTIONS TO THE DRAMA WORKSHOP

General Reactions

Ninety-four percent of respondents indicated that they had attended the drama workshop. Overall, reactions were positive, with the vast majority indicating that the workshop had exceeded their expectations (79%), had been enjoyable (86%), had held their attention (77%) and had been 'better' than the Year Nine drama workshop (80% agreement; the Year Nine drama workshop had been shorter and was held in school). Reactions to the statements on expectations, enjoyment and attention were less positive among males ($p<0.05$) and those intending to take drugs ($p<0.001$).

The overall positive response was mirrored in the focus groups. Even several weeks after the visit to the Discovery Museum, pupils recalled the workshop enthusiastically and in some detail. The sense of occasion created by the bus trip out of school, the awareness that NE Choices was unique to the city, the novelty of the workshop format and the atmospheric set design, all appeared to have created a highly memorable and stimulating experience.

> *"You felt like you were in an attic."*
> *"It was dead dark."*
> *"It was good."*
> *"Everything was painted black, even the floor."*
> *"It had atmosphere. It would have been like nothing if it was just a room like this."*
>
> (Female, Year Ten)

> *"We were told we were going on an NE Choices day trip"*
> *"It's been created for us."*
>
> (Males, Year Ten)

The more interactive nature of the workshop compared with the previous year's drama workshop was greatly appreciated.

> *"This was the best one."*
> *"No school uniform."*
>
> (Males, Year Ten)

> *"You could get more involved in this one."*
> *"It was good with the computers and the smaller groups."*
> *"You took part more."*
>
> (Females, Year Ten)

> *"I expected loads of writing and shit."*
>
> (Male, Year Ten)

The impact survey indicated that the most popular elements of the workshop were meeting the different fictional characters (the visits to character rooms), liked by 92%; watching the play (among the schools who participated in the later version), liked by 86%; and working in small groups, liked by 80%. Elements of the day which resembled more conventional learning methods, such as using the computer and Factfile and "brainstorming about the characters", were less popular, with around half saying they liked these parts of the workshop. The majority (70%) considered that the workshop was "about the right length", although approximately a fifth of intending drug users considered it too long. Observations of the drama workshop suggested that a number of pupils in each group lost concentration at several points, most notably towards the end of the morning session, and that several pupils became restless and irritable because they were not allowed to smoke anywhere in the Museum (school rules meant that pupils were not allowed to leave the museum at any point during the workshop).

Reactions to the Actors

Reactions to the Northern Stage actors were positive, with the majority (88%) agreeing that the actors encouraged pupils to speak their own minds and "understood what life is like" (83%) for people of their age. Males ($p < 0.001$) and those intending to take drugs ($p < 0.05$) were slightly less enthusiastic about the actors. However, the vast majority (84%) agreed that they paid more attention to the actors than they normally would to teachers. In the focus groups, pupils elaborated on why they found the actors compelling and credible. At the most immediate level, pupils enjoyed interacting with the actors because they were young, fashionably dressed, humorous and used realistic language ("they swore an' that!"). Beyond this, pupils relished the licence provided by the actors to engage with and challenge adult authority on an equal footing; this was particularly evident in their interactions with one of the more opinionated fictional characters, 'Paul':

> *"You could just talk to him about anything. He was really good."*
> *"Paul was canny funny. We could give him loads of stick."*
> *"He was full of crap but it was good fun."*

(Males, Year Ten)

Importantly, the actors were considered more knowledgeable and reliable sources of information on drugs than teachers, partly because of their relative youth and partly because pupils imagined they had direct personal experience.

> *"They've probably been there."*
> *"Cos they're younger. They're more like close to us."*
> *"They know what the dangers are and the effects, and how to take them...they know the social things about it..."*

(Females, Year Ten)

A final factor in pupils' engagement with the actors was a feeling that the actors treated them "with respect". This translated as meaning not only that the actors encouraged them to speak their own minds and treated their opinions as valid, but also that the actors could be trusted not to criticise or betray confidences – an important perceived difference compared with teachers.

Participation in the Workshop

The survey attempted to measure the extent to which respondents actively participated in the workshop. Responses indicated high levels of participation, with a majority answering that they had "thought of questions to ask the characters" (87%), "used the computer to get information" (84%), and taken notes about the rooms (69%). Males ($p<0.001$) and intending drug users ($p<0.001$) appeared to have participated less actively, with over a quarter in both groups indicating that other group members "did most of the work".

Identification with and Thoughts Provoked by the Fictional Characters

A series of questions in the impact survey explored reactions to and identification with the fictional characters. The characters, relatives and friends of the disappeared Rachel each represented different views on and experiences of drugs, and it was assumed that participants would relate to them in ways which reflected their own feelings about and experiences of drugs. A brief description of each character is provided in Figure 4.1.

Figure 4.1: Description on Fictional Characters

Character	Brief Description
Darren *Acquaintance of Rachel*	Local drug dealer. Witty, streetwise, 'each for himself' attitude, knowledgeable about drugs. By the end of the play the character goes clean and gets out of drug dealing.
Paul *Rachel's older brother*	Fireman. Arrogant, sexist, can't believe Rachel would be involved in drugs, thinks all drug users are "scum". Takes steroids to help his body building, is unaware of inconsistency in his views. A 'love-to-hate' character.
Emma *Rachel's best friend*	Same age as Rachel, still at school. Caring, concerned for her friend. Has limited experience of drugs (other than alcohol) and has 'stepped back' after some experimentation because frightened of consequences. Rather naïve and impressionable.
Kirsty *Acquaintance of Rachel*	Drug user, with experience of lots of substances. Is clearly under influence of drugs and behaves in a disturbing, unco-operative and alienating manner. Claims to be more confident and in control than her behaviour suggests.
Mam *Rachel's mother*	Very anxious about Rachel, naïve and fearful in relation to drugs, unsure what to do for the best as a parent. Smokes and drinks, but regards these as normal and unproblematic.

Overall, the streetwise Darren was the most popular character, identified by 63% as their favourite. Twelve percent identified Paul as their favourite and 10% Emma. Kirsty and Mam were not liked.

The impact survey also gauged how respondents reacted to and identified with the different characters (see Table 4.1). All the fictional characters appeared credible, with a majority indicating that they either knew someone like the character or could imagine meeting someone like them. Nearly a quarter (24%) said they could not imagine meeting the rather extreme drug user Kirsty, although overall she was still considered a credible character. As might be expected, identification with the characters varied in line with intending drug use: as many as 62% of intending drug users indicated that they knew someone like Darren, compared with 23% of those not intending to take drugs and 39% of respondents overall. Similarly, over a third of intending drug users (35%) indicated that they knew someone like Kirsty, compared with 14% of intended non-users and 22% overall. Intending drug users were also most likely to indicate that they knew someone like Mam.

The lower half of the table illustrates how respondents associated different attributes with the four younger characters Darren, Paul, Emma and Kirsty.

The focus groups and observations gave an insight into the kinds of issues and feelings that were triggered by visits to each of the fictional characters' rooms. Darren's room, as intended, sparked off discussion about drug dealing, particularly the extent to which supplying drugs to friends could be termed 'dealing', and the quality and purity of drugs bought from unknown sources.

> *"I'd be scared of him in case he spiked my drink or got me into drugs."*
>
> (Female, Year Ten)

Table 4.1: Reactions To and Identification with Characters

Base: All who attended the NE Choices workshop (n=975)

	Darren %	Paul %	Emma %	Kirsty %	Mam %
% Agreeing					
I know someone like (character)	39	34	49	22	51
I can imagine meeting someone like (character)	44	49	38	48	38
I cannot imagine meeting someone like (character)	13	12	7	25	6
Not sure / can't remember	3	3	5	5	3
Character is easily influenced by other people	32	31	45	61	*
Character would be fun to hang around with	65	13	53	23	*
Character is a bit of a loser	21	62	23	62	*
Character probably has a good future ahead of them	28	43	55	7	*
Character is a drug addict	54	38	14	85	*
Character will probably take drugs in the future	63	54	31	88	*
Character will probably end up in trouble with drugs	50	30	19	86	*
Character knows how to reduce the risks in taking drugs	39	32	51	17	*
Character would stand by you if you were in trouble	34	41	73	9	*

* These questions were not asked in relation to Mam

Several pupils used the visit to Darren's room to test out, display or acquire information about specific drugs. The visit to Kirsty, the problematic drug user, provided a similar opportunity for pupils to gain personally relevant information about drugs in an indirect and non-threatening way. Beyond this, however, Kirsty appeared such an extreme character that pupils found little in their visit to her room that made them think about their own lives. Her primary function in the workshop appeared to be to act as an example or warning:

> *"You could tell that Kirsty took drugs and that that's what would happen to you – she was a bit of a nutter."*
>
> (Female, Year Ten)

The visits to the three characters who had close relationships with Rachel – her friend Emma, brother Paul and Mam – focused pupils' attention on the broader social context of drug use and its effects on personal relationships. The visit to Emma's room triggered discussion of issues such as looking out for one's friends, particularly in the context of drugs, and friends growing apart (for example, some debate focused on whether Emma was the good friend to Rachel which she claimed to be, or whether she was simply jealous of Rachel's move towards drugs and growing contact with Darren and Kirsty). As expected, the visit to Mam focused attention on the issue of how much parents in general know about drugs. Mam was less successful as a device triggering pupils to consider *their own* relationship with parents, partly because, in some pupils' view, the character was too extreme and stereotypical; however, others felt that her combination of fear, ignorance and over-reaction were realistic:

> *"She always blamed herself for everything ... she was just like my Mam."*

(Male, Year Ten)

The visit to Rachel's brother, Paul, also focused attention on family reactions to suspected drug use, with several commenting that their own siblings would react similarly:

> *"If I took drugs, my brother wouldn't believe that I took drugs – that's what Paul was like."*

(Female, Year Ten)

As intended, Paul was identified as representing hypocritical views about drugs. The character triggered off a great deal of spontaneous debate, concerning his sexism, ignorance of his sister's drug-taking, stereotypical views of drug-users, and hypocrisy regarding 'acceptable' drugs such as steroids. In the last two respects, Paul appeared to function as a device encouraging pupils to raise some of the wider social and political aspects of drug use, such as social norms and double standards.

Engagement with Workshop and Thoughts Triggered About Future Drug Use

A series of attitudinal statements were used to assess the extent to which the drama workshop engaged respondents' interest and emotions and triggered them to consider their own future drug use. The results suggest that the majority of pupils engaged emotionally and intellectually with the workshop. Respondents agreed that they were stimulated to think about the different consequences of drugs (83%), the choices they make in their own lives (73%), and their own attitudes towards drugs (77%). They also engaged with the 'quest' element, with the vast majority (83%) expressing curiosity about the disappeared Rachel. Intending drug-users were, however, slightly less engaged than other respondents ($p < 0.001$).

The main cognitive impact of the workshop appeared to be in stimulating a consideration of: the importance of weighing up the risks involved in taking drugs; the risk associated with mixing drugs; the way in which others can influence your life; the difficulty in making the right choices; and the potential for people to take advantage of you if you take drugs. Around 80% or so of respondents agreed that the workshop made them think about the above issues. To a lesser extent respondents agreed that it made them think that taking drugs will always lead to trouble (65%) and that if you take drugs once you don't have to take them again (59%). General responses to this question suggest that the workshop was less likely to provoke thought amongst the intending drug users. Few (15%) reported thinking that drugs are only taken by a small proportion. Around a tenth stated that it made them feel that taking drugs is all right if you know what you are doing and that taking drugs will impress others. Agreement with these two statements was highest amongst intending drug users, with over a fifth expressing agreement (p<0.001).

The focus groups confirmed that the themes and messages most strongly communicated by the workshop were concerned with informed choice and individual decision-making. There was strong agreement that the workshop had not adopted a prescriptive anti-drugs stance:

> *"No-one on the day said, 'Don't take drugs'."*
> *"That was really good."*
> *"It wasn't like, 'This is this, don't take it.' It was more like, 'This is what happens when you take it'."*
> *"It's up to you."*
> *"Make you know about it first and then you decide."*

> (Females, Year Ten)

Pupils identified a concern with both the physical and social consequences of drugs, and alluded to the broad themes of relationships, friendships and career choices:

> *"It's more what it'll do to your life than what it'll do to your body."*
> *"It was like the effects on other people as well, to your family and friends."*

> (Females, Year Ten)

Discussion of Workshop with Others

Respondents were asked whether they had discussed the drama workshop with other people (excluding any formal discussion in the classroom). A majority had discussed the workshop with classmates (82%), with parents (72%), and with friends (60%). To a lesser extent respondents discussed the workshop with siblings (37%) and other relatives (22%). A third indicated that they had talked about the workshop with their teacher.

4.2 YOUNG PEOPLE'S REACTIONS TO THE FACTFILE

The vast majority of Year Ten pupils (91%) reported that they had received a copy of the Factfile. The impact survey measured respondents' readership, use and retention of the Factfile.

Around a quarter (24%) of respondents said they had read 'all' of the Factfile, while 43% said they had read parts of it. The vast majority had kept the file (84%), and reported to having used the file in some manner, with only 15% saying they had not used it at all. Males (p<0.01) and intending drug users (p<0.001) appeared to have lower levels of retention and usage of the file.

The Factfile seems to have been reasonably well received with the majority considering it to be easy to read (80%), liking the appearance of it (61%) and considering it to have been written by someone who understands people of their age (58%). Approximately half (48%) thought that it told you everything you need to know about drugs. A minority expressed negative views of the Factfile, considering it to be boring (15%) and stating that they would never look at it again (14%). Males (p<0.05) and intending drug users (p<0.001) were the least positive in their opinion of the Factfile.

A majority (91%) had received the CD-Rom D-Code. Nearly three-quarters (72%) had played the music tracks, but only around a third had played all or some of the drugs information game. Since the drama workshop, a tenth of respondents had visited the NE Choices website.

4.3 TEACHERS' REACTIONS TO THE YEAR TEN INTERVENTION

Teachers were involved in the Year Ten intervention both as targets (for the teacher training course) and as delivery agents (of the classroom follow-up).

The teacher training course and manual appeared to have increased teachers' knowledge and confidence regarding their ability to address drugs in the classroom.

> *"It was good, the talk about the different types, hallucinogens and things I didn't know. That prepared me 'cos I did a lesson on that."*
>
> (Teacher/Tutor)

> *"It's really important that we're bang up to date with what's going on out there otherwise the kids will reject it. There was a good balance of input from some practitioners, giving us bang up to date information."*
>
> (Co-ordinator)

> *"But having something that is well organised and constructive helps, like these packs with activities where it's all written out for you, when you've got that you don't have to do the actual preparation work, you can go at it a bit more enthusiastically."*
>
> (Year Ten Tutor)

> *"I can see the benefit of that because it wasn't preaching, it wasn't where people were told, 'Drugs are wrong and you mustn't take them'. It's obvious that kids, especially in this area, are going to come across drugs in their everyday life, a large majority of them. I think this is no-nonsense, bare-knuckle approach is probably the best way to do it, and I found that a little bit unusual but useful as well."*
>
> (Year Ten Co-ordinator)

However, some teachers felt that some of the activities in the manual adopted a more explicit approach to drugs education than their school favoured; this was more the case in the denominational schools. One or two conducted no follow-up at all because they felt drugs education had been "rammed down pupils' throats".

In organisational terms, teachers were pleased with the support provided by NDPT, particularly the provision of funding for supply cover to enable teachers to attend training. This was interpreted as a sign of genuine commitment to drugs education. Communications from NDPT were regarded as sufficient and appropriately timed. The logistical organisation of the museum drama workshops was praised.

More encouragingly, it suggests that teachers can be equipped with more confidence and skills which, even if these do not lead to immediate programme activity, may have longer-term impacts on their readiness to teach drugs education.

4.4 SUMMARY

The Year Ten intervention comprised an all-day out-of-school drama workshop that took the format of a themed quest. In addition there was classroom support and follow-up and a range of information products.

Attendance at the drama workshop was very high (94%) and overall reactions were positive. The vast majority described the workshop as enjoyable and exceeding their expectations. Qualitative research findings suggested that it was a highly memorable and stimulating experience and that pupils appreciated the interactive nature of the workshop. Reactions to the actors were positive. Pupils enjoyed interacting with the actors and perceived them to be more knowledgeable and reliable sources of information on drugs than teachers.

All the fictional characters appeared credible. Visits to the characters focused pupils attention on issues about drug dealing, family reaction to suspected drug use and on the broader social context of drug use and its effects on personal relationships. Pupils seemed to engage emotionally and intellectually with the workshop. They were stimulated to think about the different consequences of drugs, the choices they made in their own lives and their own attitudes towards drugs.

The vast majority of pupils said they had received a copy of the Factfile and that they had kept it. Around a quarter said they had read it all, while 43% said they had read bits of it. It seemed to have been reasonably well received and was considered, by most, to be easy to read.

Overall, the Year Ten intervention was positively received by the pupils although males and intending drug users gave less positive ratings at times and displayed less engagement. However, it must be noted that even among these groups response was very positive. There was little variation in response from pupils at full and partial intervention schools, suggesting that the intervention was consistently received.

Teachers were involved both as targets and delivery agents. The teacher training course and manual appeared to have increased teachers' knowledge and confidence regarding their ability to address drugs in the classroom. This may have longer-term impacts on teachers' reactions to teach drugs education.

5. REACTIONS OF YOUNG PEOPLE, YOUTH WORKERS AND PARENTS TO THE YEAR ELEVEN INTERVENTION

The Year Eleven intervention comprised a programme of youth work projects, a parents' programme, and an intervention tailored to the needs of a small group of 'high risk' young people (see Chapter 3 for more detailed information). This section examines the reactions of young people, youth workers and teachers to elements of the Year Eleven intervention. Findings are drawn from the process evaluation, which included: six focus groups with young people participating in the youth work projects; interviews with 12 of the youth workers; three focus groups with parents; interviews with the workers engaged in the high risk programme, and two focus groups with the high risk programme participants. In addition, observations were conducted of a cross-section of all activities undertaken, including the youth work projects, the parent drama session, and the residential element of the high-risk programme.

Section 5.1 discusses young people's and youth workers' reactions to the youth work projects, and Section 5.2 discusses parents' reactions to the drama sessions. Section 5.3 examines the high-risk programme, exploring both young people's and workers' reactions.

5.1 YOUTH WORK PROJECTS

Two samples of young people were interviewed, in focus groups, to explore reactions to the youth work projects:

- Project participants (four groups of Year Eleven pupils who had worked in the projects).

- Project 'target groups' (one group in Year Eleven who observed "The Wall" display produced by the project in School One, and one group of Year Nines who participated in the drama workshop produced by the School Five project).

For project participants, the experience appeared to have been enjoyable and rewarding. Initial expectations that the projects would continue many of the most enjoyable features of NE Choices – a focus on drama, engaging facilitators who treated participants "like friends" or "like adults", and access to good quality materials – were met. The NE Choices theme of informed choice appeared to have been well-absorbed:

> *"We don't say 'don't take drugs', we just say 'know that this is going to happen'."*
> *"That it's your choice, but think."*
> *"We didn't want to say no cos even if you say no they're going to do it anyway, so we made them think about it."*
> *"The thing that we were trying to get across was think about it before you do it, look at the facts."*
>
> (Year Elevens)

In addition to the drugs-related learning which occurred, participants recognised that they had gained in other ways. Some perceived improvements in their confidence and general social skills, while others pointed to project-specific skills such as art and video. One group had received a school bronze achievement award for their work on the project.

Young people who formed target groups for the projects reacted positively to the two projects involved, "The Wall" by School One and the drama workshop by School Five. There was high recall of the two projects, both of which were perceived as novel, engaging and more credible than standard classroom approaches to drugs education. The comments below are from Year Eleven participants in the youth work intervention and Year Nine pupils who were part of the drama workshop:

> *"If the teachers had done it would have been really boring."*

(Year Eleven)

> *"They were using words that we use, if they'd used other words we wouldn't have, like, got it."*
>
> *"Normally it's like 'don't take drugs'...they were telling you the consequences of doing drugs."*
>
> *"They were getting across that drugs are bad, but they were saying at the end of the day it's your life."*
>
> *"I would have thought they'd have actually said 'don't take drugs' – I was quite surprised at that."*

(Year Nines)

The youth workers perceived the young people to have gained in several ways. At the start, the six groups were perceived to vary widely in educational ability, confidence, enthusiasm, and knowledge and attitudes about drugs. In three of the projects, participants had initially been strongly anti-drug or held stereotypical views such as "drug users are bad" or "touch drugs and you end up dead". Youth workers were concerned that these naïve views would lead them to produce a peer education product that lacked credibility, and therefore spent several weeks exploring different viewpoints. Consequently, youth workers had spent more time than they had planned for on dispelling myths and building basic drugs information, before the group could begin to consider peer education ideas. As a result, several projects began with several weeks of drugs education, which slowed project development but was felt to be essential to the peer-education purpose.

> *"The biggest problem that we had was we perhaps assumed the kids' knowledge was better than it actually was...We thought they were a long way off passing the information onto other young people."*

(Youth worker)

Youth workers from all schools felt that the young people were motivated and enthusiastic. This meant that after the initial educational phase, youth workers were able to intervene less and less as the groups took greater charge of the task.

> *"I've seen a group of young women really pull it together."*

(Youth worker)

There was a need, however, to continually provide incentives to the groups, such as the residential trip and other away days, especially in times of increased pressure.

In over half of the groups, youth workers felt that participants initially experienced problems of low self-esteem and confidence, poor concentration span and communication skills. Workers described spending a great deal of time on building group coherence and confidence, and this attention to group process sometimes sat uneasily with the NE Choices' objectives, to develop a group 'product'.

The necessity to meet deadlines, to complete a project on a pre-defined issue in a specified period of time, and to deliver the project to peers, conflicted with youth worker's perceptions of peer education, which was seen to be as much concerned with the process of building relationships with young people and fostering decision-making, as with tangible outcomes. Youth workers felt that in 'real' peer education, the process would take longer than was allowed for the NE Choices, and the young people would decide their own objectives and methods, and who their peers were.

> "Peer education is about them doing it for themselves, not us saying 'you've got to do this and you need to do that'...At the beginning I felt it was the process that was more important, but the further in I got, the more the emphasis started being on the outcome. And that's not how I was sold it. I was sold it on the processes."
>
> (Youth worker)

Having said that these ideological differences existed, most youth workers were able to adjust to the suggested task and were largely comfortable with the NE Choices approach, adopting a balance that allowed aims to be met while facilitating the groups in a manner felt to be most appropriate.

> "The youth workers wanted to concentrate on the process and I think the DPI were saying yes, the process is important but we need an end product as well. So it was like that balance...to prove that we met our aims."
>
> (Youth worker)

Each project had a budget that could be used for materials or for funding external resources. Two projects invited input from community artists, two from video workers, and two from drama workers. The skills, equipment and contacts brought to the projects by the external workers were appreciated, and helped the group to develop products of a high presentational quality. However, there was also some ambivalence in most of the groups about this external input. Some groups perceived the external advisers to be pushing the project in a direction they did not like – for example, School One abandoned an initial idea for a video after buying in some video training – while others appeared to feel that the external input threatened their ownership of the project. In several projects, an increase in group coherence and clarity of ideas was observed after the external input had been 'rejected'.

Overall, youth workers felt that the projects fostered strong feelings of ownership and confidence, as well as developing specific skills such as drama, video-making and art. Against the small reach of the projects, in terms of numbers involved, must be balanced the more intensive learning. It is possible that the learning from the projects will have longer-term indirect benefits that might be disseminated informally, beyond the life span of NE Choices.

Finally, the amount of funding available for project development was found to be more than adequate for many of the groups' requirements, and youth workers felt fortunate to be able to develop a project without having concerns about going over budget.

> *"It was very well funded, very well resourced."*
> *"The funding's tremendous. The scope is just so wide...normally you've got to fight for money."*
> *"As far as money, that's been brilliant...I've never had to worry."*
>
> (Youth workers)

The funding process, while problem-free for the majority of youth workers, caused some difficulties for others in monitoring their spending, and, in particular, acquiring funds for external support from different agencies.

> *"It was just a complete nightmare trying to get money...cos people weren't employed by any particular authority...our drama worker wasn't employed by North Tyneside Council...It was such a long process for getting money."*
>
> (Youth worker)

Lack of direct access to funds was cited as one factor delaying the development of some projects.

5.2 PARENTS' PROGRAMME

This section reports parents' reactions to the drama-based drugs awareness workshops, drawing on findings from observations of the workshops and focus groups with parent attenders. It was not possible to obtain feedback from parents who had taken part in more intensive parent support groups.

As with previous NE Choices work with parents, attendance was lower than hoped, despite considerable publicity and recruitment efforts. Low turn out may have been partly attributable to parents' fear that attendance might be interpreted as their having a drugs problem in the family. Another possible factor was that, unlike in previous years of NE Choices, young people were not also involved in these drama workshops.

Parents who did attend found the workshop enjoyable and engaging.

> *"I wasn't sure myself whether it was going to be very helpful for us as parents, but it was excellent."*
> *"It was even better than the first one."*
> *"I thought it was a good approach."*
>
> (Parents)

The scenarios, characterisation and dialogue were felt to be highly realistic, and to trigger feelings of empathy and identification.

> *"There were so many different characters and personalities as well that you could relate to them and see bits of your own kids or your friends kids in there."*
>
> *"I'm sure everybody could relate in some way to one or more characters and think, 'oh yeah, that's just like so and so'."*
>
> *"I thought they were really brilliant the way they adapted."*
>
> *"These two parents were just doing exactly what we'd come up against, that sort of attitude that it wouldn't happen in their own house."*
>
> *"Certain expressions and certain ways they look, and I thought 'yes, that's the way I've seen it'."*
>
> (Parents)

Despite initial feelings of anxiety and embarrassment about participating actively in the session, parents found, to some surprise, that they enjoyed taking part:

> *"It was the one thing I was dreading and we said we'd sit at the back...But we got into it."*
>
> *"That was a surprise to me that it was going to be like that...I got carried away."*
>
> *"I wanted to get up there!"*
>
> *"I think it's much better than just being a spectator, you get more out of it."*
>
> (Parents)

The intended aims of the workshop appeared to have been largely met. Parents described gaining more of an understanding of the factors which led young people to experiment with drugs, and an appreciation of how some ways of discussing drugs with their children were more productive than others:

> *"You know, they've got pressures coming from so many different areas."*
>
> *"It did make me think more about the issues and to think that there aren't any easy answers for stopping kids doing it."*
>
> *"You can't stop them...If they're going to do it they're going to do it...Kids can get into so many different scenarios."*
>
> *"I would take a totally different approach now to what I previously would have done had I not seen that. I would have jumped straight, all guns blazing...that showed me that's not the way to tackle it...I wouldn't be quite as frightened."*
>
> (Parent)

5.3 'HIGH-RISK' YOUNG PEOPLE'S PROGRAMME

Response to the week-long Fairbridge course was very positive. Although some of the eight young people had initially attended with feelings of ambivalence and uncertainty, these concerns were quickly dispelled by the Fairbridge workers and by the generally upbeat and exciting nature of the course.

The young people were aware that the course was linked to NE Choices, due to the references made in school and on the course itself. However, it was not perceived as a drugs education course, or as being primarily concerned with drug use. Instead, there was a general understanding that the course was about giving them more confidence and offering them the opportunity to try activities which were new and challenging.

> *"To give you confidence."*
> *"To show you can do stuff."*
> *"You can do anything you want."*
>
> (Female Fairbridge participants)

Most felt that the course had succeeded in doing this. Several felt proud of their outdoor activity achievements, and frequently expressed surprise that they had ventured to try new and frightening activities. As with other NE Choices interpersonal components, the characteristics of the facilitators appeared to play a crucial and positive role in shaping response. The young people reacted positively to the Fairbridge workers, particularly the outreach worker and to former Fairbridge participants whom they met at the base.

Observations showed that the young people participated reasonably enthusiastically in the activities. There were some personality clashes and incidents which required careful handling – one female, for example, appeared to demand a lot of attention and often lost her temper. Overall, however, all the young people enjoyed being part of a group, and appreciated the freedom they were given to socialise with one another. They also appeared to enjoy the unstructured time spent at the Fairbridge base, where they felt they were "treated as clients" and equals.

There were mixed reactions to the drugs discussion session that formed part of the course. Some challenged what they felt were incorrect notions about the spiralling dangers of drug use, specifically the argument that soft drug use could lead to usage of hard drugs. Overall, however, they perceived the message of the session to have been about choice, and felt that the speaker's experiences were credible. The discussion encouraged some participants to discuss their own drug use.

> *"He sort of scared us by saying what could happen."*
> *"I suppose it's better when you actually hear it from someone who's been there and done it...than some other person with an ordinary life who's not been in that situation...He was talking the way we talk so we understood and could talk to him better."*
>
> (Female Fairbridge participants)

The young people moved on in various ways in the weeks following the course. One male enrolled in other projects run by Fairbridge, joined a student exchange programme and started a course at college. At the time of evaluation, he had moved out of his parental home, and was seen to be living successfully on his own in student accommodation. He was described as being one of Fairbridge's "stars".

> *"It's amazing, we were well chuffed with the change – quite a mature, confident young lad."*
>
> (Director)

Another male attended a Fairbridge training course in preparation for a college course, and also made occasional visits to the drop-in centre. One female decided to go to college, and three participants returned to school. One of these was also reported to be successfully holding down a summer job and was keen to move on to full time employment. Only one participant, a male, appeared to have made little progress either in educational, career or other goals.

Overall, the staff at Fairbridge felt pleased with the young people's progress. In addition, the organisation was also thought to have gained from its involvement with NDPT, particularly in developing skills to work with a group younger than its usual target population, and in raising its profile with schools.

> "Other schools have been in touch asking for opportunities. It has assisted our profile with working with that particular generation."
>
> (Director)

However, there were concerns within Fairbridge that they should not be expected to take over responsibility for tasks that were the statutory responsibility of schools. In particular, Fairbridge was anxious that young people should not be encouraged to view Fairbridge as a pleasurable alternative to school, but rather as a support which could help them to get more out of school and other aspects of life. If Fairbridge is to develop further work with young people of school age, these issues will need careful attention.

Although the young people had a range of family and school difficulties, they were perceived by Fairbridge to have fewer problems than the organisation's usual target group. Drug use appeared to be higher in the eight Fairbridge participants than in the main NE Choices cohort, although the small figures involved make it difficult to draw comparisons[2]. The Fairbridge group tended to be more likely than the full Year Eleven cohort of young people to have taken drugs, experimented with a wider range of drugs, taken more than one drug at a time and mixed drugs with alcohol.

The young people's reactions to the course were positive. They perceived the aim of the Fairbridge course to have been to give them confidence and offer them the opportunity to prove their abilities in certain tasks. This aim appeared to have been met at least in the short-term, with several expressing feelings of pride and surprise at their achievements. The boys especially enjoyed the outdoor activities while the girls liked the social aspects of the course. All respondents appeared to enjoy interacting with Fairbridge workers, whom they felt had treated them as adults.

5.4 SUMMARY

The youth work projects appeared to foster strong feelings of ownership and confidence, as well as developing specific skills such as drama, video-making and art. It is possible that the learning from the projects will have longer term indirect benefits that may be disseminated informally beyond the life span of NE Choices. Similarly, the Fairbridge intervention represents a possible model for integrating drugs prevention work with broader based personal development work with young people who are experiencing difficulties.

---

[2] The Fairbridge participants completed a modified version of he NE Choices baseline survey, in order to assess their drug experiences.

6. DRUG USE IN YOUNG PEOPLE: CROSS SECTIONAL DATA

Earlier chapters have discussed the development and implementation of NE Choices and the reaction to it. This chapter examines young people's behaviour in terms of drug taking and their potential for experiencing drug-related harm. As outlined previously (see Section 2.1), respondents were reluctant to disclose information that they felt could lead to them being identified and, consequently, the level of successful matching of respondents between baseline and follow-up surveys was low. Data are therefore presented in two chapters to reflect two approaches to analysis. Chapter 7 presents data relating to the cohort of pupils who could be matched between the baseline and the third follow-up survey. This cohort comprises 1,036 pupils, equivalent to 54% of the original baseline sample. This limited data set is analysed to determine whether any change by intervention level can be attributed to the NE Choices programme. This chapter presents the results from varying numbers of subjects across the four surveys. These data provide a useful description of drug-related behaviour of young people in separate age groups. However, due to the threat of bias posed by sample attrition, their use in estimating progress against outcome measures by intervention level is problematic. Confidence intervals are provided to indicate the extent of variation in prevalence estimation in each survey.

This chapter reports background information on the sample characteristics (6.1) and exposure to drug offers (6.2) before addressing the prevalence of drug use (6.3) and patterns of drug use (6.4).

6.1 CHARACTERISTICS OF SAMPLE

Table 6.1 shows the characteristics of the sample. Throughout the surveys the sample has comprised a slightly higher proportion of females than males. Two thirds or more of respondents in each sample indicated that they lived with both their parents. More than three-quarters indicated that at least one parent worked full-time or both worked part-time. This proportion was highest in the final survey (86%). At baseline a quarter were current smokers rising to around a third in the follow-up surveys while weekly drinking rose from 28% to over half (56%). Almost half (48%) at baseline indicated that they had close friends who had taken drugs. This peaked at over two-thirds (69%) at the second follow-up but reduced to 62% at the third follow-up. Intentions to take drugs seemed to increase at the first and second follow-up but diminished again at the third follow-up. Throughout the tables in this chapter, the results show similar reductions in several measures. These include, for example, lifetime experience of drug offers and lifetime prevalence of drug experimentation, which technically should not reduce in later surveys. Possible explanations for the reductions shown by the data are:

- sample attrition, whereby non-respondents at the final survey were those who previously reported higher prevalence, earlier onset of drug experimentation and more frequent use.

- changes in administration of the survey, whereby some respondents may have been reluctant to disclose drug use when their answers could potentially be traced back to them.

Table 6.1: Characteristics of Sample

Base	Baseline 1936 %	1st Follow-up 1751 %	2nd Follow-up 1579 %	3rd Follow-up 1429 %	Baseline 95% Confidence Interval %	1st Follow-up 95% Confidence Interval %	2nd Follow-up 95% Confidence Interval %	3rd Follow-up 95% Confidence Interval %
Gender								
Male	48	43	43	45	(46, 51)	(41, 46)	(40, 45)	(43, 48)
Female	50	53	52	55	(48, 52)	(51, 55)	(49, 54)	(52, 57)
Live with both natural parents	69	69	67	70	(67, 71)	(67, 71)	(65, 70)	(67, 72)
At least one parent in full-time or both in part-time work	79	83	83	86	(77, 81)	(81, 85)	(81, 85)	(84, 87)
Current smoker	25	32	36	33	(23, 27)	(30, 35)	(34, 39)	(31, 35)
Weekly drinker	28	39	51	56	(26, 30)	(37, 41)	(48, 53)	(53, 58)
Close friends drug use	48	61	69	62	(46, 50)	(58, 63)	(67, 72)	(59, 64)
Intentions re. drugs								
Definitely not	40	33	30	47	(38, 42)	(30, 35)	(28, 32)	(45, 50)
Possibly	51	51	51	44	(48, 53)	(48, 53)	(49, 53)	(41, 46)
Definitely yes	10	17	19	9	(8, 11)	(15, 19)	(17, 21)	(7, 10)

Base: All respondents (Baseline n=1936, 1st Follow-up n=1751, 2nd Follow-up n=1579, 3rd Follow-up n=1429)

6.2 EXPOSURE TO DRUG OFFERS

This measure was included to provide background information on the potential availability of drugs.

Pupils were asked to read through a list of drugs and indicate whether they had ever been in a situation where they were offered these drugs or could have had some if they wanted to. Almost a half (47%) to three-quarters (71%) of respondents at various survey sweeps indicated that they had been in such a situation (Table 6.2). The number of drugs offered ranged from an average of 1.6 at baseline to 3.0 at the second follow-up, reducing to 2.4 at the third follow-up.

Cannabis was the drug most commonly cited as being offered, ranging from almost a third (32%) to two-thirds (66%). These young people seemed to have access to a range of drugs. Up to a third indicated that they had been offered or had the opportunity to obtain amphetamines, poppers and solvents and up to around a quarter indicated offers of LSD and magic mushrooms. Cocaine, heroin, and tranquillisers had been offered or were available to around a tenth or more. Response on the two dummy drugs, mensomine and nadropax, suggests that around four percent and two percent respectively at the second and third follow-ups may have provided false details about drug offers. False reports are not necessarily due to dishonesty but could easily represent respondents' confusion concerning drugs on offer. The low response to these fictitious drugs suggests that there was limited over-reporting within each survey. A fairly substantial proportion, peaking at 14% at the first follow-up, stated that a drug was offered but they were unsure what the drug was, further confirming that pupils were not always fully aware of the drugs on offer.

Table 6.2: Exposure to Drug Offer Situation

Base	Baseline 1936 %	1st Follow-up 1751 %	2nd Follow-up 1579 %	3rd Follow-up 1429 %	Baseline 95% Confidence Interval %	1st Follow-up 95% Confidence Interval %	2nd Follow-up 95% Confidence Interval %	3rd Follow-up 95% Confidence Interval %
Any drugs offered	47	62	71	66	(45, 49)	(60, 65)	(69, 73)	(63, 68)
Speed/Amphetamines	13	21	31	28	(12, 15)	(19, 23)	(29, 34)	(25, 30)
Cannabis	32	53	66	61	(30, 34)	(51, 55)	(63, 68)	(59, 64)
Cocaine	6	8	12	11	(5, 7)	(7, 9)	(10, 14)	(10, 13)
Ecstasy	10	15	20	20	(9, 12)	(14, 17)	(18, 22)	(18, 22)
Heroin	5	6	9	5	(4, 6)	(5, 8)	(8, 10)	(4, 6)
Ketamine	1	3	4	3	(1, 2)	(2, 4)	(3, 5)	(2, 3)
LSD	15	23	27	19	(13, 16)	(21, 25)	(24, 29)	(17, 21)
Magic Mushrooms	16	23	26	17	(14, 17)	(21, 25)	(24, 28)	(16, 19)
Mensomine	–	2	4	2	–	(2, 3)	(3, 5)	(1, 3)
Nadropax	1	3	4	2	(1, 2)	(2, 3)	(3, 5)	(1, 3)
Poppers/Nitrites	13	26	30	23	(12, 15)	(24, 28)	(28, 32)	(21, 25)
Solvents	26	36	37	26	(24, 28)	(34, 39)	(34, 39)	(24, 29)
Tranquillisers	8	15	16	11	(7, 9)	(13, 17)	(14, 18)	(10, 13)
Offered a drug but unsure what it was	13	14	13	9	(11, 14)	(13, 16)	(11, 15)	(8, 11)
Some other drug was offered	1	3	3	1	(1, 2)	(2, 4)	(2, 4)	(1, 2)
Mean number of drugs offered	1.6	2.5	3.0	2.4	(1.5, 1.7)	(2.4, 2.7)	(2.9, 3.2)	(2.2, 2.6)

Base: All respondents (Baseline n=1936, 1st Follow-up n=1751, 2nd Follow-up n=1579, 3rd Follow-up n=1429)

Throughout the surveys, the majority of those who had been offered drugs indicated that the offer had been made in the open-air (Table 6.3). It seems that as these respondents have grown older they have been exposed to drugs in a range of places, with an increase between the baseline and final surveys in the proportions indicating drug offers at parties, a friend's house, a pub or club, an older person's house or school. Fewer than 10% had been exposed to drug offers at home.

Table 6.4 illustrates the source of the drug offer. Throughout the surveys, friends and acquaintances have been the main source of drug offers, accounting for around a half of all drug offers. Around a quarter or more at each survey stage indicated that their drug offer was made by a stranger, while relatives accounted for less than 10% of drug offer sources.

Table 6.3: Location of Drug Offer

Base	Baseline 914 %	1st Follow-up 1092 %	2nd Follow-up 1121 %	3rd Follow-up 937 %	Baseline 95% Confidence Interval %	1st Follow-up 95% Confidence Interval %	2nd Follow-up 95% Confidence Interval %	3rd Follow-up 95% Confidence Interval %
Open air somewhere	60	65	66	58	(57, 63)	(62, 68)	(64, 69)	(55, 61)
A party	30	40	46	48	(27, 33)	(37, 43)	(43, 49)	(45, 51)
A friend's house	23	35	46	42	(20, 25)	(32, 38)	(43, 49)	(38, 45)
An older person's house or flat	19	25	29	21	(17, 22)	(22, 27)	(26, 32)	(19, 24)
School	12	21	25	26	(10, 14)	(19, 24)	(22, 27)	(23, 29)
Home	6	7	8	4	(4, 8)	(5, 8)	(6, 9)	(3, 6)
A pub or club	7	16	25	35	(5, 9)	(14, 19)	(22, 27)	(32, 38)
Other	7	5	5	5	(5, 9)	(4, 6)	(3, 6)	(3, 6)
Not sure	2	1	1	1	(1, 3)	(1, 2)	(0, 1)	(0, 1)
Not stated	10	5	3	2	(8, 12)	(4, 7)	(2, 4)	(1, 3)

Base: All who have been around when drugs have been offered (Baseline n=914, 1st Follow-up n=1092, 2nd Follow-up n=1121, 3rd Follow-up n=937)

Table 6.4: Source of Drug Offer

Base	Baseline 914 %	1st Follow-up 1092 %	2nd Follow-up 1121 %	3rd Follow-up 937 %	Baseline 95% Confidence Interval %	1st Follow-up 95% Confidence Interval %	2nd Follow-up 95% Confidence Interval %	3rd Follow-up 95% Confidence Interval %
Friends	42	58	61	59	(39, 45)	(55, 61)	(59, 64)	(56, 62)
Someone you know but not a friend or relative	43	47	51	56	(39, 46)	(44, 50)	(48, 54)	(53, 59)
Someone you did not know	32	24	27	28	(29, 35)	(22, 27)	(24, 29)	(25, 31)
Relative(s)	6	7	10	7	(4, 7)	(6, 9)	(8,11)	(5, 8)
Other	1	2	3	2	(1, 2)	(1, 3)	(2, 4)	(1, 3)
Not sure	2	2	2	1	(1, 2)	(1, 3)	(1, 2)	(1,2)
Not stated	11	6	3	2	(9, 12)	(5, 7)	(2, 4)	(1, 3)

Base: All who have been around when drugs have been offered (Baseline n=914, 1st Follow-up n=1092, 2nd Follow-up n=1121, 3rd Follow-up n=937)

6.3 PREVALENCE OF DRUG USE

This section addresses drug use at three levels:

- lifetime experimentation with drugs (the proportion of young people who have ever tried);

- drug 'use', defined as having tried a drug, taken it within the past six months and holding definite intentions to take that drug again, and

- 'regular use', calculated as having tried a drug, taken it six or more times in the previous six months and holding definite intentions to take that drug again.

In addition, intended future use of drugs, although not an outcome measure, is reported.

Ever Use of Drugs

Table 6.5 displays the proportion of respondents who indicated that they had tried drugs or solvents and the types tried.

At the baseline survey, around a third (34%) of pupils indicated that they had tried drugs. At the first follow-up the proportion having tried drugs was 45% and then 53% by the second follow-up survey. However, the final survey showed the proportion as having 'ever tried drugs' was 40%. This pattern is consistent with the inference of sample attrition being a major influence on the reporting of prevalence.

Throughout the research, cannabis was the main drug to have been tried, reported by between over a fifth (22%) to almost a half (48%) of respondents. Solvents also seemed to be popular, tried by a fifth at baseline and rising to over a quarter (26%) in the first two follow-up surveys. Pupils seemed to have tried a range of drugs, with reported drug trying generally peaking at the second follow-up before showing a reduction in the final survey. At the second follow-up, around a fifth had tried amphetamines (18%) and nitrites (20%), but this reduced to around a tenth (11%) by the final survey. LSD and magic mushrooms had been tried by more than a tenth at the second follow-up, but reduced to five percent by the final survey. At the final survey, experimentation with cocaine, ecstasy and tranquillisers reduced to less than five percent, while heroin, ketamine and the fictitious drugs mensomine and nadropax had been tried by less than one percent. The low response to the fictitious drugs throughout the research suggests that there has been little over-reporting.

The lower part of Table 6.5 summarises drug experimentation into the proportions that had tried cannabis only, tried cannabis, solvents and nitrites only and tried drugs other than these. It is evident that experimentation has not been limited to cannabis, with a higher proportion having tried other substances than cannabis alone.

Table 6.5: Prevalence of Drug Trying

Base	Baseline 914 %	1st Follow-up 1092 %	2nd Follow-up 1121 %	3rd Follow-up 937 %	Baseline 95% Confidence Interval %	1st Follow-up 95% Confidence Interval %	2nd Follow-up 95% Confidence Interval %	3rd Follow-up 95% Confidence Interval %
Tried any drug	34	45	53	40	(31, 36)	(43, 48)	(51, 55)	(37, 42)
Speed/Amphetamine	6	13	18	11	(5, 8)	(11, 14)	(16, 20)	(9, 12)
Cannabis	22	38	48	37	(20, 24)	(36, 40)	(46, 50)	(34, 39)
Cocaine	2	3	5	3	(2, 3)	(3, 4)	(4, 6)	(2, 4)
Ecstasy	3	5	8	4	(2, 4)	(4, 6)	(6, 9)	(3, 5)
Heroin	2	2	4	<1%	(1, 2)	(1, 3)	(3, 4)	(0, 1)
Ketamine	1	1	2	<1%	(0, 1)	(0, 1)	(1, 3)	(0, 1)
LSD	6	12	13	5	(5, 8)	(10, 13)	(12, 15)	(4, 6)
Magic Mushrooms	9	13	13	5	(8, 10)	(11, 15)	(12, 15)	(4, 6)
Mensomine	n/a	1	2	<1%	–	(0, 1)	(1, 3)	(0, 1)
Nadropax	1	1	2	<1%	(0, 1)	(0, 1)	(1, 3)	(0, 1)
Poppers/Nitrites	8	16	20	11	(7, 9)	(14, 18)	(18, 22)	(10, 13)
Solvents	20	26	26	14	(19, 22)	(24, 28)	(24, 28)	(12, 15)
Tranquillisers	5	9	9	4	(4, 5)	(7, 10)	(8, 11)	(3, 5)
Taken a drug but unsure what it was	4	4	5	2	(3, 5)	(3, 5)	(4, 6)	(1, 3)
Tried cannabis only	6	9	15	17	(5, 7)	(8, 11)	(13, 17)	(15, 19)
Tried cannabis, solvents or nitrites only	16	21	27	25	(14, 18)	(19, 23)	(25, 29)	(23, 27)
Tried other than cannabis, solvents or nitrites	16	23	25	14	(14, 18)	(21, 25)	(23, 27)	(12, 15)

Base: All respondents (Baseline n=1936, 1st Follow-up n=1751, 2nd Follow-up n=1579, 3rd Follow-up n=1429)

Table 6.6 illustrates the number of different drugs that respondents indicated they had tried. Between the baseline and the second follow-up the results show not only that the prevalence of drug experimentation increased but also that the number of drugs experimented with increased from a mean of two to three.

The third follow-up survey revealed a higher level of non-experimentation (60%), and, among those who had tried drugs, the mean number of drugs experimented with reduced to about two-and-a-half. Thus, the responses at the third follow-up most closely resembled the baseline responses. This reduction is possibly due to sample attrition or the change in the survey administration mode.

Table 6.6: Number of Different Drugs (Including Solvents) Indicated as Having Tried

Base	Baseline 1936 %	1st Follow-up 1751 %	2nd Follow-up 1579 %	3rd Follow-up 1429 %
None	66	55	47	60
One	13	14	19	19
Two	8	10	10	8
Three	4	6	6	5
Four	3	4	4	2
Five or more	5	11	14	6
Mean number of different drugs tried	2.67 (95% C.I. 2.50, 2.80)	3.16 (95% C.I. 2.99, 3.33)	3.29 (95% C.I. 3.10, 3.48)	2.46 (95% C.I. 2.28, 2.63)

Table 6.7 displays drug 'use' which, for each drug, has been computed as having tried the drug, taken it in the previous six months and holding definite intentions to take that drug again. At baseline less than a tenth (7%) were categorised as 'users' rising to almost a fifth (17%) by the second follow-up survey. At each survey cannabis was the main drug used, peaking at 15% at the second follow-up.

Table 6.7: Prevalence of Drug 'Use'

Base	Baseline 1936 %	1st Follow-up 1751 %	2nd Follow-up 1579 %	3rd Follow-up 1429 %	Baseline 95% Confidence Interval %	1st Follow-up 95% Confidence Interval %	2nd Follow-up 95% Confidence Interval %	3rd Follow-up 95% Confidence Interval %
Use any drug or solvent	7	15	17	7	(6, 8)	(13, 16)	(15, 19)	(6, 9)
Speed/Amphetamines	1	3	4	1	(0, 1)	(2, 3)	(3, 5)	(1, 2)
Cannabis	5	13	15	7	(4, 6)	(11, 15)	(14, 17)	(5, 8)
Cocaine	<1%	<1%	1	1	(0, 0)	(0, 1)	(1, 2)	(0, 1)
Ecstasy	1	1	2	1	(0, 1)	(0, 1)	(1, 3)	(1, 2)
Heroin	<1%	<1%	1	0	(0, 0)	(0, 0)	(0, 1)	(0, 0)
Ketamine	<1%	<1%	<1%	<1%	(0, 0)	(0, 0)	(0, 1)	(0, 0)
LSD	1	3	2	<1%	(0, 1)	(2, 3)	(2, 3)	(0, 1)
Magic Mushrooms	1	3	2	1	(1, 2)	(2, 4)	(2, 3)	(0, 1)
Mensomine	–	<1%	<1%	<1%	–	(0, 1)	(0, 0)	(0, 0)
Nadropax	<1%	<1%	<1%	<1%	(0, 0)	(0, 1)	(0, 1)	(0, 0)
Poppers/Nitrites	1	4	2	1	(1, 2)	(3, 5)	(1, 3)	(1, 2)
Solvents	2	3	3	<1%	(2, 3)	(3, 4)	(2, 3)	(0, 1)
Tranquillisers	1	2	2	1	(0, 1)	(1, 3)	(1, 2)	(0, 1)
Use of cannabis only	3	7	9	4	(2, 3)	(6, 8)	(7, 10)	(3, 5)
Use of cannabis, solvents or nitrites only	4	9	11	5	(3, 5)	(8, 11)	(9, 12)	(4, 6)
Use other than cannabis, solvents or nitrites	2	5	6	3	(2, 3)	(4, 6)	(5, 7)	(2, 3)

Base: All respondents (Baseline n=1936, 1st Follow-up n=1751, 2nd Follow-up n=1579, 3rd Follow-up n=1429)

Table 6.8 displays 'regular use' which, for each drug, has been computed as having tried the drug, taken it six or more times in the previous six months and holding definite intentions to take that drug again. Regular drug use was low at baseline (4%) rising to 13% by the second follow-up. Once again the final survey showed levels of regular use similar to those of the baseline sample. Cannabis was the drug most commonly linked to regular use.

TABLE 6.8: Prevalence of 'Regular Drug Use'

Base	Baseline 1936 %	1st Follow-up 1751 %	2nd Follow-up 1579 %	3rd Follow-up 1429 %	Baseline 95% Confidence Interval %	1st Follow-up 95% Confidence Interval %	2nd Follow-up 95% Confidence Interval %	3rd Follow-up 95% Confidence Interval %
Regular use of any drug	4	11	13	5	(3, 5)	(9, 12)	(11, 14)	(4, 6)
Speed/Amphetamines	<1%	1	2	1	(0, 0)	(1, 2)	(1, 2)	(0, 1)
Cannabis	3	9	12	5	(2, 4)	(8, 11)	(10, 13)	(4, 6)
Cocaine	<1%	<1%	1	<1%	(0, 0)	(0, 1)	(0, 1)	(0, 0)
Ecstasy	<1%	<1%	1	1	(0, 0)	(0, 1)	(0, 1)	(0, 1)
Heroin	<1%	<1%	<1%	0	(0, 0)	(0, 0)	(0, 1)	(0, 0)
Ketamine	0	<1%	<1%	<1%	(0, 0)	(0, 0)	(0, 0)	(0, 0)
LSD	<1%	1	1	<1%	(0, 1)	(1, 2)	(1, 2)	(0, 0)
Magic Mushrooms	<1%	1	1	<1%	(0, 0)	(1, 2)	(1, 2)	(0, 1)
Mensomine	–	<1%	0	<1%	–	(0, 0)	(0, 0)	(0, 0)
Nadropax	0	<1%	<1%	0	(0, 0)	(0, 0)	(0, 0)	(0, 0)
Poppers/Nitrites	1	2	1	1	(0, 1)	(1, 2)	(0, 1)	(0, 1)
Solvents	1	2	2	<1%	(1, 2)	(2, 3)	(1, 2)	(0, 0)
Tranquillisers	<1%	1	1	<1%	(0, 1)	(1, 2)	(0, 1)	(0, 1)
Regular use of cannabis only	2	6	8	3	(1, 2)	(5, 7)	(7, 10)	(2, 4)
Regular use of cannabis, solvents or nitrites only	3	8	9	4	(2, 4)	(7, 9)	(8, 11)	(3, 5)
Regular use other than cannabis, solvents or nitrites	1	3	3	1	(0, 1)	(2, 3)	(3, 4)	(1, 2)

Base: All respondents (Baseline n=1936, 1st Follow-up n=1751, 2nd Follow-up n=1579, 3rd Follow-up n=1429)

Recent Use of Drugs

Respondents who had tried any drugs or solvents were asked to indicate when they had last taken any. This question caused difficulty for some respondents who were unable to accurately recall when they had last taken drugs or solvents. Table 6.9 illustrates the reported recency with which drugs or solvents were taken.

Throughout the research, the majority of those who had tried drugs or solvents indicated they had taken them in the six months prior to the survey. At baseline, fewer than a fifth (16%) had taken drugs or solvents in the previous week, but the first and second follow-up surveys displayed more recent use, with more than a quarter having taken drugs in the preceding week. The third follow-up results indicated the least recent drug taking, with over two-fifths (43%) having stated that it was more than six months since they had taken drugs or solvents. Table 6.10 displays recent use of drugs or solvents as a proportion of all survey respondents.

Table 6.9: When Last Took Drugs or Solvents

Base	Baseline 650 %	1st Follow-up 793 %	2nd Follow-up 837 %	3rd Follow-up 566 %	Baseline 95% Confidence Interval %	1st Follow-up 95% Confidence Interval %	2nd Follow-up 95% Confidence Interval %	3rd Follow-up 95% Confidence Interval %
In the last week	16	27	26	13	(13, 19)	(24, 30)	(23, 29)	(11, 16)
In the last month	18	18	18	14	(15, 21)	(15, 20)	(16, 21)	(11, 17)
In the last 3 months	12	10	9	11	(9, 14)	(8, 12)	(7, 11)	(8, 13)
In the last 6 months	16	13	14	16	(14, 19)	(11, 16)	(12, 17)	(13, 19)
More than 6 months ago	24	25	26	43	(21, 27)	(22, 28)	(23, 29)	(39, 47)
Not sure	7	4	4	2	(5, 9)	(3, 6)	(2, 5)	(1, 3)
Not stated	7	3	3	1	(5, 9)	(2, 4)	(2, 4)	(0, 2)

Base: All who have tried any drugs or solvents (Baseline n=650, 1st Follow-up n=793, 2nd Follow-up n=837, 3rd Follow-up n=566)

TABLE 6.10: Recency of Taking Drugs or Solvents

Base	Baseline 1936 %	1st Follow-up 1751 %	2nd Follow-up 1579 %	3rd Follow-up 1429 %	Baseline 95% Confidence Interval %	1st Follow-up 95% Confidence Interval %	2nd Follow-up 95% Confidence Interval %	3rd Follow-up 95% Confidence Interval %
Taken drugs or solvents	34	45	53	40	(31, 36)	(43,48)	(51, 55)	(37, 42)
Not in last 6 months	8	11	14	17	(7, 9)	(10,13)	(12, 16)	(15, 19)
In last 6 months	21	31	36	21	(19, 23)	(29,33)	(33, 38)	(19, 23)
In last 3 months	15	25	28	15	(14, 17)	(23,27)	(26, 30)	(13, 17)
In last month	12	20	23	11	(10, 13)	(18,22)	(21, 26)	(9, 12)
In last week	5	12	14	5	(4, 6)	(11,14)	(12, 16)	(4, 6)
Not sure when taken last	5	3	3	1	(4, 6)	(2, 4)	(3, 4)	(1, 2)

Base: All respondents (Baseline n=1936, 1st Follow-up n=1751, 2nd Follow-up n=1579, 3rd Follow-up n=1429)

At each survey stage at least a fifth of all respondents indicated that they had taken drugs or solvents in the preceding six months. This peaked at the second follow-up survey, with over a third (36%) having done so.

Intended Future Use of Drugs

Respondents were asked to indicate their intentions to take or not to take various drugs. The response categories comprised a four-point scale of: 'definitely will not take'; 'probably will not take'; 'probably will take'; 'definitely will take' and 'not sure'. These have been recoded to 'definitely not', 'possibly' and 'definitely will' to provide a simpler variable. The 'possibly' category comprises the 'probably not', 'probably will' and 'not sure' responses. Table 6.11 shows the proportions indicating the different intentions concerning use of any drugs or solvents.

Table 6.11: Intended Future Use of Drugs or Solvents

Base	Baseline 1936 %	1st Follow-up 1751 %	2nd Follow-up 1579 %	3rd Follow-up 1429 %	Baseline 95% Confidence Interval %	1st Follow-up 95% Confidence Interval %	2nd Follow-up 95% Confidence Interval %	3rd Follow-up 95% Confidence Interval %
Definitely not	40	33	30	47	(38, 42)	(30, 35)	(28, 32)	(45, 50)
Possibly	51	51	51	44	(48, 53)	(48, 53)	(49, 53)	(41, 46)
Definitely yes	10	17	19	9	(8, 11)	(15, 19)	(17, 21)	(7, 10)
Not sure when taken last	5	3	3	1	(4, 6)	(2, 4)	(3, 4)	(1, 2)

Base: All respondents (Baseline n=1936, 1st Follow-up n=1751, 2nd Follow-up n=1579, 3rd Follow-up n=1429)

At the baseline survey around half of the respondents (51%) indicated a possibility that they would take drugs or solvents in the future and a tenth conveyed definite intentions to do so. Intentions to take drugs seemed to become more positive by the first and second follow-up surveys, with almost a fifth expressing definite intentions to take drugs at both surveys. The third follow-up survey shows the highest proportion reporting a definite intention not to take drugs and the lowest proportion stating a definite intention to take drugs. This is likely to be because those most likely to take drugs did not respond to the final survey.

Intended future use of drugs was strongly associated with past use, with definite intentions to use drugs highest among those who had previously tried drugs and statistically significant at baseline and each follow-up (p<0.001). Thus, those who had tried drugs in the past consistently expressed greater intention to take drugs in the future (Table 6.12).

Table 6.12: Intended Future Use of Drugs or Solvents By Previous Drug Trying

Base	Baseline Whether tried drugs		1st Follow-up Whether tried drugs		2nd Follow-up Whether tried drugs		3rd Follow-up Whether tried drugs	
	Yes 650 %	No / not sure 1286 %	Yes 793 %	No / not sure 958 %	Yes 837 %	No / not sure 742 %	Yes 566 %	No / not sure 863 %
Definitely not	15	52	12	49	11	51	25	62
Possibly	62	45	53	49	55	46	54	37
Definitely yes	23	3	35	2	34	2	21	1

Base: All respondents (Baseline n=1936, 1st Follow-up n=1751, 2nd Follow-up n=1579, 3rd Follow-up n=1429)

Table 6.13 shows combined responses of 'definite' and 'probable' intentions to take drugs and provides an indication of perceived likelihood of taking each drug in the future. Intended drug taking was highest at the first and second follow-up surveys, where more than a third considered it likely that they would take cannabis and more than a tenth reported likelihood of taking speed, LSD, magic mushrooms, poppers or solvents. Five percent or more indicated intentions to take cocaine, ecstasy or tranquillisers. Intended use of heroin and ketamine was particularly low and was at a similar level as that reported for the dummy drugs mensomine and nadropax. The third follow-up survey showed a reduction in both 'definite' and 'probable' intentions to take most drugs. For example, only a quarter expressed intentions to take cannabis and less than a tenth (7%) intended taking amphetamines.

Table 6.13: Definite and Probable Intention to Use Drugs or Solvents

Base	Baseline 1936 %	1st Follow-up 1751 %	2nd Follow-up 1579 %	3rd Follow-up 1429 %	Baseline 95% Confidence Interval %	1st Follow-up 95% Confidence Interval %	2nd Follow-up 95% Confidence Interval %	3rd Follow-up 95% Confidence Interval %
Speed/Amphetamines	8	13	15	7	(7, 9)	(11, 14)	(13, 17)	(5, 8)
Cannabis	21	33	37	25	(19, 23)	(31, 35)	(35, 39)	(23, 27)
Cocaine	4	5	5	3	(3, 5)	(4, 6)	(4, 6)	(2, 4)
Ecstasy	6	7	7	4	(5, 7)	(6, 8)	(6, 8)	(3, 5)
Heroin	3	3	3	<1%	(3, 4)	(2, 4)	(3, 4)	(0, 1)
Ketamine	2	2	3	1	(2, 3)	(1, 3)	(2, 3)	(0, 1)
LSD	9	11	11	3	(8, 10)	(9, 12)	(10, 13)	(2, 4)
Magic Mushrooms	10	12	11	3	(8, 11)	(11, 14)	(9, 13)	(2, 4)
Mensomine	–	2	3	<1%	–	(2, 3)	(2, 3)	(0, 1)
Nadropax	2	2	3	1	(2, 3)	(2, 3)	(2, 4)	(0, 1)
Poppers / Nitrites	7	12	12	5	(6, 8)	(11, 14)	(10, 14)	(4, 6)
Solvents	12	12	10	2	(10, 13)	(10, 13)	(9, 12)	(2, 3)
Tranquillisers	6	8	8	3	(5, 7)	(7, 9)	(7, 9)	(2, 3)

Base: All respondents (Baseline n=1936, 1st Follow-up n=1751, 2nd Follow-up n=1579, 3rd Follow-up n=1429)

6.4 PATTERNS OF DRUG USE

This section examines patterns of drug use including age of first use, frequency of use and the use of drugs in combination with other drugs and alcohol.

Age of First Drug Use

Table 6.14 displays age of first experimentation with drugs or solvents as a proportion of all respondents.

Table 6.14: Age at First Drug or Solvent Trying Experience

Base	Baseline 1936 %	1st Follow-up 1751 %	2nd Follow-up 1579 %	3rd Follow-up 1429 %	Baseline 95% Confidence Interval %	1st Follow-up 95% Confidence Interval %	2nd Follow-up 95% Confidence Interval %	3rd Follow-up 95% Confidence Interval %
Tried any drug or solvents	34	45	53	40	(31,36)	(43,48)	(51,55)	(37,42)
Age 11 or under	6	6	7	n/a	(5, 7)	(5, 7)	(5, 8)	(n/a)
Age 12 (or under #)	12	9	8	4	(10, 13)	(8, 10)	(6, 9)	(3, 6)
Age 13	12	15	13	8	(11, 14)	(13, 17)	(11, 15)	(7, 9)
Age 14	1	13	14	11	(1, 2)	(11, 14)	(12, 16)	(9, 12)
Age 15	–	1	10	10	–	(1, 2)	(8, 11)	(8, 11)
Age 16	–	–	1	6	–	–	(0, 1)	(5, 7)
Age 17	–	–	–	<%	–	–	–	(0, 0)
Not sure / not specified	2	2	2	1	(2, 3)	(1, 2)	(1, 2)	(0, 1)

Base: All respondents (Baseline n=1936, 1st Follow-up n=1751, 2nd Follow-up n=1579, 3rd Follow-up n=1429)
3rd Follow-up scale ranged from 'age 12 or under' to 'age 17'

The majority of respondents were aged 13 years at the baseline, 14 at the first follow-up, 15 at the second follow-up and 16 at the third follow-up. The results are reasonably consistent between the first three surveys, with the slight variation in reported age of first use likely to be a consequence of respondents' difficulty in recall and sample fluctuations. Overall it appears that a minority (6%) of young people first experimented with drugs at age 11 or under. Each year thereafter it seems that around a tenth or more (ranging from 8% to 15%) experimented with drugs for the first time. Thus, at the time of the second follow-up survey slightly under half the sample had never tried drugs and a further tenth or so had only recently experimented for the first time.

In the final survey the proportions who indicated that they had tried drugs at age 12 or under or age 13, reduced considerably to only four percent and eight percent respectively. Given the higher rates of young drug experimentation reported at earlier stages it appears that many of those who had tried drugs at age 13 or under did not participate in the final survey. The results show that around six percent of the final survey respondents had first experimented with drugs at age 16 or 17.

FREQUENCY OF DRUG USE

For each drug they had tried, respondents were asked to indicate how often, if at all, they had tried each in the six months prior to the survey. Table 6.15 displays the results.

Table 6.15: Most Frequent Use of Any Drugs or Solvents in Last 6 Months

Base	Baseline 650 %	1st Follow-up 793 %	2nd Follow-up 837 %	3rd Follow-up 566 %	Baseline 95% Confidence Interval %	1st Follow-up 95% Confidence Interval %	2nd Follow-up 95% Confidence Interval %	3rd Follow-up 95% Confidence Interval %
None	24	23	24	41	(20, 27)	(20, 25)	(21, 27)	(37, 45)
Once	24	18	16	18	(21, 28)	(16, 21)	(13, 18)	(15, 22)
2-5 times	20	20	21	16	(17, 23)	(17, 23)	(18, 24)	(13, 19)
6-10 times	8	9	9	7	(6, 10)	(7, 11)	(7, 11)	(5, 9)
More than 10 times	12	23	24	15	(10, 15)	(20, 25)	(21, 27)	(12, 18)
Not sure / not specified	12	7	6	3	(10, 15)	(5, 9)	(4, 7)	(2, 5)

Base: All who have tried drugs or solvents (Baseline n=650, 1st Follow-up n=793, 2nd Follow-up n=837, 3rd Follow-up n=566)

There seemed to be a wide variation in the frequency of drug taking among those who had tried drugs or solvents and also some difficulty in reporting frequency, with many unsure or not specifying their frequency. Within the first three surveys, around a quarter of those who had tried drugs or solvents had not taken any in the preceding six months. Around a fifth had only taken them once in that period, while a similar proportion had done so between two and five times. The first two follow-up surveys suggested that by Year Ten and Eleven drug taking had become more frequent, with almost a quarter having taken drugs or solvents more than ten times in the preceding six months. However, the third follow-up survey revealed less frequent drug and solvent use with an increase to over two-fifths (41%) not having taken any and a decrease to 15% in those having taken them over ten times in the six months prior. Thus it would seem that the more frequent drug takers might have been less likely to participate in the final survey. A comparison of frequency of drug use by survey stage and gender is presented in Table 6.16. Females generally reported less frequent drug use than males, although this was only significant at the second follow-up (p<0.05).

Table 6.16: Most Frequent Use of Any Drugs or Solvents in Last 6 Months By Survey Stage and Gender

	Baseline		1st Follow-up		2nd Follow-up		3rd Follow-up	
	Male 290 %	Female 345 %	male 324 %	Female 425 %	Male 337 %	Female 441 %	Male 221 %	Female 345 %
None	24	24	24	22	25	25	40	42
Once	26	24	14	23	13	17	19	18
2-5 times	16	22	18	20	18	23	14	16
6-10 times	8	8	9	11	9	9	6	7
More than 10 times	14	10	27	19	30	18	18	13
Not stated	12	12	9	5	4	7	2	4

Base: All who have tried any drugs or solvents (Baseline n=650, 1st Follow-up n=793, 2nd Follow-up n=837, 3rd Follow-up n=566)

USE OF DRUGS IN COMBINATION WITH OTHER DRUGS

Table 6.17 displays data on the use of multiple drugs at the same time (poly-drug use). It seems that within the six months preceding each survey, a minority of those who had experimented with drugs or solvents had engaged in poly-drug use. While just over one in ten (12%) experimenters reported recent poly-drug use at the baseline, this increased to around a fifth in the subsequent follow-up surveys. The frequency of poly-drug use seemed to increase also. At each of the follow-up surveys approximately one-tenth of experimenters had engaged in poly-drug use on three or more occasions in the previous six months.

USE OF DRUGS IN COMBINATION WITH ALCOHOL

Drinking alcohol with drugs or solvents seemed to be more prevalent than poly-drug use, with nearly a third reporting this at baseline, increasing to two-fifths or more in subsequent follow-ups (Table 6.18). While between 16% and 19%, at each survey stage, reported taking alcohol together with drugs or solvents only once in the previous six months, a substantial proportion had done so on a number of occasions. Among those who had taken alcohol along with drugs or solvents, the frequency increased from an estimated average of around two times in the preceding six months at baseline to an average of three times or more at the follow-up stages.

Table 6.17: Whether, In Last 6 Months, Have Taken More Than One Drug at the Same Time

	Baseline 650 %	1st Follow-up 793 %	2nd Follow-up 837 %	3rd Follow-up 566 %
No	80 (95% C.I. 76, 83)	76 (95% C.I. 73, 79)	73 (95% C.I. 70, 76)	83 (95% C.I. 80, 86)
Yes	12 (95% C.I. 9, 14) 19	19 (95% C.I. 16, 22) 20	20 (95% C.I. 17, 23) 16	16 (95% C.I. 13, 19)
Once	6	7	6	6
Twice	2	2	3	2
Three times	1	3	3	2
Four times	1	2	2	1
Five times	1	1	1	1
Six times	<1%	<1%	1	1
Seven times or more	1	3	4	4
Not sure	2	2	1	1
Not stated	6	3	5	1
Estimated mean number of times	2.17 (95% C.I. 1.78, 2.57)	3.04 (95% C.I. 2.69, 3.39)	3.38 (95% C.I. 3.04, 3.72)	3.32 (95% C.I. 2.81, 3.83)

Base: All who have tried any drugs or solvents (Baseline n = 160, 1st Follow-up n = 793, 2nd Follow-up n = 837, 3rd Follow-up n = 566)

Table 6.18: Whether, In Last 6 Months, Have Drunk Alcohol Together with Taking Drugs or Solvents

	Baseline 650 %	1st Follow-up 793 %	2nd Follow-up 837 %	3rd Follow-up 566 %
No	61 (95% C.I. 57, 65)	52 (95% C.I. 48, 55)	48 (95% C.I. 44, 51)	58 (95% C.I. 54, 62)
Yes	30 (95% C.I. 27, 34)	43 (95% C.I. 40, 46)	48 (95% C.I. 44, 51)	40 (95% C.I. 36, 44)
Once	16	18	19	16
Twice	4	6	8	5
Three times	4	6	5	5
Four times	2	3	3	4
Five times	<1%	2	2	1
Six times	1	2	1	1
Seven times or more	2	6	9	6
Not sure	4	2	1	1
Not stated	5	3	3	1
Estimated mean number of times	2.29 (95% C.I. 2.03, 2.56)	2.87 (95% C.I. 2.64, 3.09)	3.01 (95% C.I. 2.78, 3.23)	2.91 (95% C.I. 2.62, 3.19)

Base: All who have tried any drugs or solvents (Baseline n = 160, 1st Follow-up n = 793, 2nd Follow-up n = 837, 3rd Follow-up n = 566)

6.5 SUMMARY

The baseline survey achieved a response rate of 87%. The final survey was administered by post and achieved an approximate response rate of 64%. The sample attrition, and possibly the change to a postal methodology, seemed to have the effect of reducing the reported drug prevalence at the final survey. It appears that non-respondents were more likely to have experimented with drugs, done so more frequently and initiated experimentation at a younger age.

The available data have been analysed by intervention level in two ways. First, by comparing full intervention, partial intervention and control schools. Second, by comparing those schools receiving any level of the intervention (full and partial) with the control schools. Due to the very large number of statistical tests, a prevalence of null findings, and a loss to follow-up of early drug users that introduced bias into the sample, the details of the analysis are not presented. Drug taking behaviour was similar across the different levels of intervention and between intervention and control respondents. Therefore, there did not appear to be any evidence that NE Choices, or the different levels of delivery of NE Choices (full and partial), had impacted on drug prevalence or harm reduction as intended.

However, the cross-sectional data provides a rich description of drug experiences in successive year cohorts. The majority of young people had been exposed to drug offer situations. They seemed to have access to a range of drugs, but particularly cannabis, with as many as two-thirds having been offered or having had the opportunity to obtain this. More than half had experimented with drugs. Cannabis was the main drug to have been tried although many had tried amphetamines, nitrites, solvents, LSD and magic mushrooms. A minority of drug experimenters (peaking at a fifth) had, in the six months prior to the survey, taken more than one drug at the same time. Taking drugs in combination with alcohol was more prevalent, with nearly half the experimenters having done so.

Secondary outcome measures on parent-child communication about drugs and experience of harmful effects from drug taking were also collected and analysed, although not presented within this chapter. Recency and theme of parent-child communication about drugs did not appear to have been impacted by the intervention, nor did the proportion of experimenters who had experienced what they perceived to be a 'bad experience' from drugs. These secondary outcome measures were, however, difficult measures to collect as parent-child communication about drugs could be infrequent and informal and perceptions of what entailed a 'bad experience' could vary between respondents.

7. OUTCOME EVALUATION ON DRUG USE AMONG YOUNG PEOPLE: ANALYSIS OF MATCHED SAMPLES

As it was not possible to match all respondents between survey stages, the previous chapter presented responses from the full sample at each individual survey stage. While drug taking changed as the pupils grew older, it did not vary significantly by intervention level at each survey stage. Thus it yields no evidence of the NE Choices programme, or the different levels of NE Choices (full and partial), having impacted on drug prevalence or harm reduction as intended. This chapter examines a sub-group of the original sample – a cohort of 1,036 pupils (equivalent to 54% of the original baseline sample and 72% of the third follow-up sample) – whose responses could be matched between the baseline and the final survey. Other survey sweeps have been compared, but the baseline versus the final survey compares the largest number of matched individuals. Also, other matched comparisons do not show any evidence of effect from NE Choices and they are not included in this report.

7.1 CHARACTERISTICS OF SAMPLE

Table 7.1 shows the characteristics of the cohort of young people whose responses could be matched between the baseline and third follow-up survey. The *responses* of the cohort (i.e. intentions to take drugs) at the third follow-up reflect those of the full sample quite well (see Table 6.1). However, their baseline *characteristics* differ from those of the full baseline sample. In particular, the matching cohort were less likely at baseline to have been current smokers, weekly drinkers or have close friends who had taken drugs, and were more likely, than the full baseline sample, to have been female and to live with both their natural parents. The cohort, therefore, is not representative of the original baseline sample. Despite this, there is value in examining this cohort to understand how they changed throughout the research period and to see if there is any indication of an impact from NE Choices on this particular group.

At baseline, there were no significant differences in the characteristics of the matched sample according to allocation to full or partial intervention or control group. However, at the third follow-up the full intervention cohort contained the highest proportion of smokers while the partial intervention cohort contained the highest proportion of weekly drinkers.

The limited matching between these surveys makes it impossible to identify the characteristics of non-respondents at the final survey. However, the differences between the full baseline sample and the baseline results for the matched cohort have implications for judging the effectiveness of the programme. They suggest that those in the third follow-up who did not provide details of matching identifiers or who did not return the questionnaire were more likely to be current smokers, weekly drinkers and to have close friends who had taken drugs. Therefore, non-response is likely to account for the reduction in reported drug taking at the final survey (see Section 6.1).

Table 7.1: Characteristics of Sample By Survey Stage By Intervention Level

Base	Baseline				3rd Follow-up			
	Total 1036 %	Full 311 %	Partial 338 %	Control 387 %	Total 1036 %	Full 311 %	Partial 338 %	Control 387 %
Gender								
Male	44	44	46	42	44	44	46	42
Female	56	56	54	58	56	56	54	58
Live with both natural parents	77	77	75	79	72	75	69	73
At least one parent in full-time or both in part-time work	82	84	83	79	89	89	90	88
Current smoker	17	20	15	20	30	36	26	28*
Weekly drinker	21	23	21	20	53	47	59	53**
Close friends drug use	40	37	42	40	60	59	60	60
Intentions re. drugs								
Definitely not	45	45	48	43	49	51	47	50
Possibly	48	47	49	49	43	44	44	42
Definitely yes	6	8	4	7	7	5	9	9

* $p<0.05$, ** $p<0.01$

Base: All respondents in sample matching between Baseline and 3rd follow-up (n=1036)

7.2 PREVALENCE OF DRUG USE

Table 7.2 shows, for the baseline and third follow-up survey, reported drug experimentation, use and regular use of any drug, cannabis only, cannabis solvents or nitrites only or other drugs, analysed by level of intervention. While the proportion having tried, used and regularly used each of these increased between the baseline and the third follow-up, the increase appeared to be consistent across all levels of the intervention with no variation evident at the third follow-up.

The cohort's drug taking behaviour, as reported in the third follow-up survey, was compared against their baseline reports to establish the stability or direction of change in their drug taking status. Table 7.3 shows that, for the majority of the cohort (68%) their drug taking status remained unchanged with over half (56%) remaining non-triers of drugs. Around a tenth (11%) remained triers only, while fewer than one percent had been users at baseline and remained so by the final follow-up. The main direction of change was in progression to drug taking with more than a fifth (22%) having progressed. This progression principally comprised experimentation with 17% having moved from being a non-trier to a trier. A smaller proportion (4%) progressed from non-trier or trier to use of cannabis, solvents or nitrites only. Only one percent progressed further, to use of harder drugs. A very small proportion (2%) appeared to de-escalate their drug taking by changing from use of harder drugs to use of cannabis, solvents or nitrites only or to non-use of any drugs. Almost one in ten (8%) provided inconsistent reports by indicating drug trying at baseline and then at the follow-up indicating not having tried. This may have resulted from reluctance to disclose drugs behaviour, judging a drug taking incidence as too limited or too far in the past to be worthy of mention or realisation that the drug tried was not what it was previously thought to have been.

Table 7.2: Prevalence of Drug Trying, Use and Regular Use By Survey Stage By Intervention Level

Base	Baseline				3rd Follow-up			
	Total 1036 %	Full 311 %	Partial 338 %	Control 387 %	Total 1036 %	Full 311 %	Partial 338 %	Control 387 %
Drug Trying								
Any drug	24	26	25	22	36	39	34	35
Cannabis only	5	5	5	4	16	15	16	16
Cannabis, solvents or nitrites only	14	14	14	13	25	24	23	26
Other than cannabis, solvents or nitrites	9	10	9	7	11	14	10	9
Drug Use								
Any drug	3	5	2	2	6	5	6	7
Cannabis only	1	3	1	1	3	3	3	5
Cannabis, solvents or nitrites only	2	4	1	2	4	4	4	5
Other than cannabis, solvents or nitrites	1	1	1	1	1	1	2	1
Regular Use								
Any drug	1	2	1	1	4	3	4	5
Cannabis only	1	2	<1	1	3	2	2	4
Cannabis, solvents or nitrites only	1	2	1	1	3	2	3	4
Other than cannabis, solvents or nitrites	0	0	0	0	1	<1	1	1
Base: All who have tried any drugs or solvents and are in sample matching between Baseline and 3rd Follow-up (Baseline n=249, 3rd Follow-up n=372)								
Mean number of drugs tried	1.97	1.98	2.13	1.88	2.24	2.47	2.32	1.96

Base: All respondents in sample matching between Baseline and 3rd follow-up (n=1036)

Table 7.3: Stability of Drug or Solvent Taking Status of Cohort From Baseline to 3rd Follow-up

Base	Total 1036 %	Full 311 %	Partial 338 %	Control 387 %
Remained Stable	68	66	68	68
Remained non-trier	56	53	57	57
Remained trier	11	13	11	10
Remained user	<1	<1	1	1
Progressed	22	21	22	24
To tried drugs	17	17	16	18
To user of cannabis, solvents or nitrites only	4	3	3	5
To user of drugs other than cannabis, solvents or nitrites	1	1	2	1
De-escalation	2	4	1	1**
No longer using drugs other than cannabis, solvents or nitrites	<1	1	<1	1
No longer using cannabis, solvents or nitrites	1	3	1	1
Inconsistent				
Tried at baseline but indicated not tried at 3rd follow-up	8	8	9	7

** $p < 0.01$
Base: All respondents in sample matching between Baseline and 3rd follow-up (n=1036)

With the exception of de-escalation of drug use, the results were consistent for the different levels of intervention. Respondents from full intervention schools reported the highest incidence of de-escalation, with four percent (equivalent to 12 respondents) doing so compared to only one percent (three respondents) at partial and one percent (four respondents) at control schools. While the numbers and proportions involved are small, this data suggests that NE Choices may have encouraged these full intervention respondents to de-escalate their drug use.

Table 7.4 shows the stability and direction of change in the cohort's intentions to take drugs. For over half (56%) there was no change between baseline and the third follow-up in their intentions concerning drug taking. Around a fifth (21%) developed greater intentions to take drugs while almost a quarter (23%) developed diminished intentions to take drugs. Results were similar for the different levels of intervention, suggesting that NE Choices did not impact on intended drug use.

7. OUTCOME EVALUATION ON DRUG USE AMONG YOUNG PEOPLE: ANALYSIS OF MATCHED SAMPLES

Table 7.4: Change in Intentions to Take Drugs or Solvents

Base	Total 1036 %	Full 311 %	Partial 338 %	Control 387 %
Greater intention to take drugs	21	19	25	19
No change in intention to take drugs	56	55	56	58
Lesser intention to take drugs	23	26	20	23

Base: All respondents in sample matching between Baseline and 3rd follow-up (n=1036)

7.3 PATTERNS OF DRUG USE

Age of First Experimentation with Drugs

Table 7.5 shows the reported age of first drug use at each survey stage. The base for these calculations is the number claiming to have tried any drugs or solvents at each stage. At the baseline there was no significant variation by intervention level. By the third follow-up survey respondents from full intervention schools reported the youngest age of first experimentation (p<0.01). However, closer examination of the data reveals that respondents from partial and control schools seemed less inclined to report the same young age of initial drug taking that they had reported at baseline.

Frequency of Drug Taking

Table 7.6 shows the most frequent use of any drug, among those who had tried any drugs or solvents. Full intervention respondents reported the least frequent drug use at the follow-up (p<0.05) with half not having taken any in the previous six months. However, partial intervention respondents reported the most frequent use, which suggests that the difference is not due to any intervention effect.

Table 7.5: Age of First Drug or Solvent Trying Experience By Survey Stage By Intervention Level

| Base | Baseline | | | | 3rd Follow-up | | | |
	Total 1036 %	Full 311 %	Partial 338 %	Control 387 %	Total 1036 %	Full 311 %	Partial 338 %	Control 387 %
Age 11 or under	14	11	10	20	n/a	n/a	n/a	n/a
Age 12 (or under #)	35	37	33	35	10	15	11	4
Age 13	43	44	48	36	22	26	18	21
Age 14	4	5	2	4	24	28	18	26
Age 15	0	0	0	0	25	19	24	31
Age 16	0	0	0	0	18	12	25	17
Age 17	0	0	0	0	1	0	1	1
Not stated	6	4	7	6	1	0	3	1
Mean rank (Lower rank = younger age of first use)		122	125	107		156	199	198

3rd Follow-up scale ranged from 'age 12 or under' to 'age 17'
Base: All who have tried any drugs or solvents and are in sample matching between Baseline and 3rd Follow-up (Baseline n=249, 3rd Follow-up n=372)

Table 7.6: Most Frequent Use of Any Drugs or Solvents in Last 6 Months By Survey Stage By Intervention Level

| Base | Baseline | | | | 3rd Follow-up | | | |
	Total 1036 %	Full 311 %	Partial 338 %	Control 387 %	Total 1036 %	Full 311 %	Partial 338 %	Control 387 %
None	26	22	24	32	40	50	27	41
Once	29	27	29	31	21	18	24	20
2–5 times	22	27	24	17	17	16	21	15
6–10 times	5	7	5	2	6	5	7	7
More than 10 times	6	4	8	7	13	9	14	15
Not stated	11	13	10	11	3	2	7	1
Mean rank (Lower rank = Less frequent use)		117	116	100		160	200	181

Base: All who have tried any drugs or solvents and are in sample matching between Baseline and 3rd Follow-up (Baseline n=249, 3rd Follow-up n=372)

Use of Drug in Combination with other Drugs

Among those who had tried drugs and solvents (n= 249 at baseline and n = 372 at third follow-up), the proportion having used a drug in combination with another drug in the previous six months was seven percent at baseline and 13% at the third follow-up. There was no significant difference by intervention level.

Use of Drugs in Combination With Alcohol

Among those who had tried drugs (n= 249 at baseline and n = 372 at third follow-up), the proportion having used a drug and consumed alcohol at the same time, within the previous six months was 22% at baseline and 40% at third follow-up. The matched sample slightly under-represents the occurrence of mixing alcohol and drugs reported in the baseline sample. Analysis of the matched sample by intervention level within each survey stage revealed no significant variation by intervention level.

7.4   SUMMARY

There was a reluctance among many respondents to disclose information that could potentially identify them and, as a result, the level of successful matching between baseline and follow-up surveys was low. Consequently, it is not possible to say conclusively whether or not NE Choices had an effect on levels of drug use.

A cohort, comprising 54% of original baseline respondents, was matched to the final survey. This cohort was not representative of the full baseline sample and, for example, under-represented prevalence of drug experimentation, smoking and weekly drinking. However, the cohort provided an opportunity to examine transitions in drug taking status. Over half (56%) remained non-triers of drugs between the baseline and third follow-up survey, while over a fifth (22%) progressed into drug experimentation or use. A very small proportion (2%) appeared to reduce their drug use by moving away from harder drugs to taking cannabis, solvents or nitrites only or no drugs. Progression of drug taking did not vary by intervention level but respondents from full intervention schools reported the highest levels of de-escalation of drug use (4%). While the numbers and proportions are very small, the data suggests that, within the matching cohort, NE Choices may have encouraged full intervention respondents to reduce their drug use. However, it is not possible, due to the level of matching, to identify whether or not the full sample showed the same transition in their drug taking.

Given the low matching between survey stages it is not possible to say conclusively whether or not NE Choices impacted upon drug taking behaviour as intended. However, the analysis of the reduced cohort does not provide any evidence of impact on drug taking behaviour for any of the outcome variables.

8. CONCLUSIONS

This is the second of two DPAS reports describing the development, implementation and evaluation of NE Choices, a three-year multi-component drugs prevention intervention for adolescents in the north-east of England. The first report (Stead et al 2000) outlined the history and theoretical basis of NE Choices and the development and implementation of the first year of intervention. It also presented data on young people's reactions to the first year, and on baseline drug use. This second report continues the story, describing the development and implementation of the second and third years of intervention, and reactions to them by young people, teachers, youth workers and parents.

The report also presents final results from the outcome evaluation of NE Choices, which measured drug use at baseline and at three points afterwards, the final being one year after the last intervention phase, the Year Eleven intervention. An experimental design was used, comparing a cohort who participated in NE Choices with a comparison cohort drawn from four schools in neighbouring geographical areas that did not receive NE Choices.

NE Choices was a social influences programme, designed to equip young people with the information and skills to make informed and safer choices about drug use. It used a mix of interpersonal, media and other components targeted on young people, the primary target, and at secondary targets of parents, teachers, school governors, youth workers, the local media and the local community.

The mix, type and targeting of components changed each year in response to the changing needs and interests of the various target groups. For example, the Year Nine intervention (the first year) had at its core a drama workshop delivered in school to the universal Year Nine population. The workshop communicated messages concerned both with prevention and harm reduction. In Year Ten, the core component similarly targeted the universal Year Ten population, but was delivered out of school on the assumption that this would have greater credibility and appeal to an older age group. A greater emphasis was placed on harm reduction messages, in response to the target group's increased exposure to drugs. The third year of NE Choices, the Year Eleven intervention, moved completely out of school with intensive youth work for self-selecting groups of peers and a selective programme specifically targeting 'high risk' young people. Systematic ongoing formative and process research was used to provide continual feedback and guidance on how to modify the programme. For example, media-based information products were revised each year to reflect changing drug trends and the growing maturity of the target group.

Both reports provide compelling qualitative and quantitative evidence that NE Choices was a credible and engaging intervention for young people and for other secondary target groups such as parents. The drama-based components in Year Nine and Year Ten triggered an overwhelmingly positive response, confirming previous research that the 13-16 age group is receptive to drama as a medium for drugs prevention. If target groups do not find interventions enjoyable, engaging, credible and memorable, they are unlikely to be receptive to learning from them (eg. Denman et al 1995, Bouman et al 1998, Orme & Starkey 1998). NE Choices appears to provide a template for creating the conditions in which drugs prevention learning can take place among 13-16 year olds. Furthermore, even young people disaffected with school and at high risk of drug use engaged with the intervention through the Year Eleven Fairbridge programme for high-risk young people. Parents who participated in the intervention in Years Nine and Eleven reported increases in drugs knowledge, an improved understanding of why young people take drugs, and greater appreciation of how best to discuss drugs with their children. Teachers and youth workers gained in drugs knowledge and drugs education skills through their participation in NE Choices training and their hands-on experience of delivering parts of the NE Choices intervention.

In terms of drug use outcomes, the intervention does not appear to have been associated with changes in drug behaviour. Drug use prevalence levels, age of onset, and frequency of use were similar in intervention and comparison groups throughout and at the final survey.

A key question is therefore why, despite evidence of considerable success in engaging its target group, the evaluation provides no evidence that the NE Choices intervention had an impact on drug use. There are a number of possible explanations, falling into three broad categories: flaws in the evaluation methods used, flaws in intervention design, and flaws in intervention delivery. These are discussed below.

(i)   Methodological flaws

The sample size was insufficient.

When a trial fails to achieve an impact on key outcome measures, the sample size and power may be called into question. Resources to implement and evaluate NE Choices were limited, meaning that the evaluation could only be implemented in six evaluation schools with a total initial sample size set at 1936 pupils. Recent literature has emphasised the importance of differentiating sampling arranged on the basis of either individuals or *clusters*. When an intervention is administered to and may impact upon clusters of subjects, such as young people within a school, it is the number of clusters (schools) that should be the basis of sample size calculation and data analysis (Kerry & Bland 1998, Ukoumunne et al 1999). Subjects within a cluster cannot be considered independent as subjects within a cluster will be more alike than subjects from different clusters (Bland & Kerry 1997, Roberts & Sibbald 1998). Bland and Kerry (1997) warn that not conducting analysis at the cluster level may lead to spurious *positive* findings. The absence of cluster analysis in the evaluation of NE Choices, therefore, does not affect the conclusion of null effect on main outcome measures. However, it means that we should treat the findings on de-escalation of drug use with caution.

Differential response to the longitudinal surveys led to inconclusive results.

The difficulties experienced with matching pupils' responses have obfuscated the analysis. The sensitive nature of the data being collected meant that pupils, particularly those who had experimented with drugs, were often reluctant to disclose the initial of their first name and their date of birth to allow their responses to be matched at each stage. As a result it was not possible to analyse results for a complete cohort. The cross-sectional analysis and the analysis of the small cohort that could be matched did not provide evidence of impact. It is not possible to infer what the results might have shown had the full cohort been analysed.

Interpretation of the final results was further complicated by sample attrition and the change to a postal administration at the final survey. While the response rate was very high it appears that non-respondents at the final survey may have been more likely to have previously reported higher prevalence, earlier onset of drug experimentation and more frequent use. It is also possible that some of the apparent reductions in drug use evident at the last survey were a result of reluctance among some respondents to disclose drug use information when their answers could potentially be traced back to them.

(ii)   Flaws in Theoretical Basis and Concept

The social influences approach was inappropriate.

One possible explanation for the apparent lack of impact of NE Choices is that the choice of social influences as the intervention approach was inappropriate. Although evidence has emerged since the intervention to suggest that large social influences interventions may be ineffective at preventing smoking (Peterson et al 2000), at the time of designing the intervention there was sufficient evidence to suggest that social influences is a powerful approach for preventing substance use (Ellickson et al 1993a, Ellickson et al 1993b, Botvin et al 1990, Botvin et al 1995, Pentz et al 1989, Pentz & Valente 1993). For example, evaluation of the Midwestern Prevention Project, or Project STAR, found reductions of up to 40% in marijuana use and daily smoking, with smaller reductions in alcohol use, which were sustained up to grade 12 (the last year of high school) (Pentz et al 1989, Johnson et al 1990, Pentz et al 1997).

(iii)   Inappropriate Targeting

NE Choices should have targeted a younger group.

Despite the evidence in support of the social influences approach cited above, the approach has usually been implemented with younger age groups (e.g. 10-13), rather than with 13-16 year olds. It was noted during the NE Choices development period that the social influences approach was largely untested with the 13-16 year old age group (Stead et al 2000). It is possible that while social influences may be an appropriate and effective approach for younger adolescents, it is less appropriate and powerful with older adolescents. At the time of planning NE Choices, there were no local drug use prevalence data available, and decisions about programme design and targeting were taken on the basis of studies from elsewhere in the UK. When NE Choices baseline data became available, a year into the intervention, local drug use prevalence and age of first onset appeared higher than had been anticipated before the intervention. This meant that, in hindsight, NE Choices might have been delivered too late in young people's lives to have a meaningful impact on their drug use, as many were already experimenting with drugs. Future interventions with prevention goals may be more appropriately targeted at young people in the pre-experimentation stage, which appears on the basis of current data to be around age 11.

A further difficulty with designing interventions for the 13-16 year old age group is that it appears to be harder to engage the parents of secondary school pupils than primary school parents, who tend to have a broader involvement in the life of the school.

(iv)   Insufficiently Intensive

NE Choices was not delivered for long enough or intensely enough to have an impact.

Although in UK terms NE Choices appears a large and intensive programme, it is worth noting that it compares poorly in terms of length and intensity to most of the social influences interventions tested in the USA. For example, the school component of the five-year Project STAR comprised between 10 and 13 classroom sessions, followed up by five booster sessions. These classroom sessions were supported by parent and child homework and parent 'organisation', community organisation, development of drug policy, and mass media work (Pentz et al 1989, Johnson et al 1990, Pentz et al 1997). The Life Skills Training (LST) programme comprised 15 classroom sessions in Year One and 15 'booster' sessions over the following two school years (Botvin et al 1990).

NE Choices, even when optimally implemented, was less intensive. The core Year 9 component was a two to three hour drama workshop, plus classroom follow-up varying from one to four hours. The core Year Ten component was a five to six hour drama workshop, plus classroom follow-up ranging from one to eight hours. In Year Eleven, those young people who did not participate in the six month-long youth work projects or the 'high risk' programme in Year Eleven, would have received around two to four hours of NE Choices, from classroom follow-up and from viewing the youth work projects when they were delivered in the schools. A small number of young people would have participated much more intensively, in the youth work projects and the Fairbridge programme.

For the majority of the NE Choices cohort, then, their total exposure to NE Choices over the intervention period would have ranged between 11 and 25 hours, with the majority receiving around 15 hours, assuming that they participated in the core elements of the Year Nine drama workshop and classroom follow-up (see Stead et al 2000) and in the Year Ten drama workshop and classroom follow-up. This was a lower intervention 'dosage' than that achieved in Project STAR and Life Skills Training. It is therefore possible that despite NE Choices' appeal and theoretically sound basis, there simply wasn't enough of it to impact on behaviour. Resource constraints, and the political requirement to deliver the intervention in other schools across Northumbria in addition to the six evaluation schools, diluted the amount of funding available for each school. Although NDPT gained considerable added value through in-kind support and sponsorship, which enabled the intervention to develop and deliver high quality information products, a prevention trial requires a realistic amount of funding for management, development, implementation and evaluation if it is to have adequate strength and integrity. In retrospect, it appears that the resources for NE Choices could have been spread too thinly.

In addition, curriculum constraints, particularly in Years Ten and Eleven when pupils are preparing for exams, would have made it difficult to deliver more classroom follow-up than was negotiated with the schools. Issues involved in working in secondary schools are discussed further below.

(v)   Insufficiently different

There was insufficient difference between the NE Choices intervention and the drugs education delivered in comparison schools.

Another possible explanation might lie in the nature of the drugs education delivered in the comparison schools over the intervention period. It is important to emphasise that the comparison school respondents did not act strictly as controls in that, rather than receiving *no* drugs intervention, they would have received 'drugs education as normal'. As part of the process evaluation, interviews were conducted with relevant teaching staff in three of the four comparison schools (it was not possible to arrange an interview in the fourth school) in an attempt to gauge the nature and intensity of this drugs education.

The amount of drugs education offered to Year Nine to Eleven pupils varied. In one school, a six-week structured programme of an hour a week in Year Ten was delivered, while in another school the drugs education amounted to two one-hour lessons, also delivered in Year Ten. The third school provided around two hours in Year Nine, and around an hour each in Years Ten and Eleven. All three schools provided a mixture of information about the nature and effects of specific drugs and discussion about why people take drugs and how to deal with drug-related situations. On average, the three schools provided around four hours of drugs education over three years to the Year Nine to Eleven cohort. In comparison, as noted above, the majority of the NE Choices cohort would have received an average of around 10 hours, although the small numbers who took part in the youth work projects and the 'high risk' programme would have received far more.

Methods used in the comparison schools included talks, discussion, watching videos, card games, and some input from outside speakers (the police or local youth workers). In one school, some Year Nine pupils had devised a short play about drugs which was then performed in a local primary school. The aims of the drugs education offered in the three schools were broadly similar, and consistent with NE Choices: to provide accurate and credible information about drugs, and to encourage young people to think about the consequences and how they might handle drug offer or drug use situations. Overall, however, the drugs education in the comparison schools appeared to have been less intensive than NE Choices, and also to have been less interactive, consisting largely of whole class discussion and videos. While the impact of this drugs education on comparison school respondents cannot be estimated, it does nonetheless appear that there was a reasonable difference in scale and intensity between the drugs education offered in comparison schools and that provided in the NE Choices evaluation schools.

(vi)   Inappropriate Delivery Methods

NE Choices delivered inappropriate activities and products, and/or delivered them via ineffective agents.

Another possible explanation is that the delivery methods used in NE Choices were inappropriate. However, there is little evidence to support this explanation. As noted above, the target groups appeared to be highly receptive to the use of drama as a medium for drugs prevention. Furthermore, the drama workers, and in Year Eleven the youth workers, were consistently and overwhelmingly rated as credible, engaging, and attractive.

Several guidelines advocate that teachers should be the prime delivery agent for drugs education throughout primary and secondary school. In NE Choices, drama workers and youth workers delivered the main components, although classroom teachers were supported, with training, materials and advice, to deliver classroom follow-up programmes. It could be argued that all or more of the programme should have been delivered by teachers (as was the case in Project Star and LST, successful social influences programmes). This might have embedded NE Choices more firmly and sustainedly in the school curriculum, thereby increasing its impact. Against this it could be argued that the intervention would have been less memorable and less credible without the involvement of actors and youth workers who, time and time again, were rated as more credible, empathetic and in-touch by the young people. Another benefit of using 'external' delivery agents rather than teachers is that they ensure greater consistency of delivery. Even where teachers were supported by a standardised NE Choices training programme and a resource manual, there were still wide variations in the amount and type of follow-up which was conducted, both between and within schools. The process evaluation findings suggest that there may be limits to the adoption and delivery of standardised, centralised drugs prevention in schools.

(vii) Poor Implementation

The intervention was well designed but poorly implemented.

One explanation for the apparent lack of effect of some prevention programmes is that, despite a sound design, they are not implemented correctly or consistently in real life conditions (e.g. Nutbeam et al 1993a). This is an argument for paying careful attention to implementation processes. However, the NE Choices process evaluation indicated that, overall, the programme was implemented as planned. Drama and youth work elements were delivered to a high standard across sites and participant groups in all three years. Where there were apparent weaknesses, these were in the classroom follow-up, which was patchy and inconsistent at Year Nine, and less intensive than anticipated in some schools at Year Ten. Implementation weaknesses may provide some of the explanation for NE Choices' lack of impact, but probably form only a small part of the picture.

(viii) Insufficient 'Community' Involvement

NE Choices would have been more effective if complemented and reinforced by a comprehensive programme of community involvement.

In NE Choices, a multi-component intervention was developed in which core interpersonal components – the drama workshops and youth work projects – were supported with media activity, information products, support and activities for parents, and training and advice for teachers and school governors. The links between intervention elements appear to have produced some beneficial effects: for example, the appeal and credibility of information products seemed to be enhanced through association with the drama workshops; the provision of materials and activities for both parents and young people gave both a shared platform for discussing drug use, and the teacher training stimulated teachers to conduct at least some classroom follow-up, thereby prolonging the life of the drama workshops in the classroom.

In addition, there was some 'community' involvement in NE Choices. The intervention included a 'mapping' of community networks, to identify the most appropriate channels for: accessing parents, workshops and support groups for parents, promotional and press work targeting the local media, and input by representatives of key statutory services in the intervention communities through a steering group.

However, the intervention was not intended to be a multi-faceted community programme. This was because the DPI was already conducting a trial of an integrated community programme, also in the north of England (Bucke et al [Eds.], forthcoming publication). It is possible that more sustained and systematic efforts to build community awareness of and support for the intervention could have both increased parental participation in the intervention and also strengthened the intervention's effects on young people. However, this kind of work is long-term and intensive, and could not have been carried out within NE Choices as it was originally conceived.

Overall, the most likely explanation for the lack of evidence that NE Choices had an impact on young people's drug behaviour is a combination of factors. Firstly, the difficulties experienced in matching respondents in the outcome evaluation severely restricted the analysis of results. This, combined with the sample attrition meant that the outcome evaluation was inconclusive. Neither cross-sectional nor longitudinal (matched) data showed any evidence of impact from the intervention.

Secondly, the intervention was insufficiently intensive. Although large by UK standards, NE Choices was less intensive than some of the major US-based trials of social influences and substance use prevention programmes. Weak intensity was compounded by the limited and patchy classroom follow-up, although the process evaluation suggests that there are limits to how much classroom follow-up secondary schools may be able to offer, even when provided with standard training and resource materials, given the demands on the secondary school curriculum. Thirdly, with hindsight it seems that young people may have been too old when first entering the NE Choices intervention, and that it may have been more appropriate to target eleven to fourteen year-olds – the age range usually targeted by social influences programmes.

A number of lessons for future drugs prevention research and practice emerge from the NE Choices evaluation:

Design of interventions

- Interventions should be of sufficient length and intensity to stand a chance of impacting on behaviour. This means delivering a similar intervention 'dosage' to that achieved in the large social influences and life skills prevention trials in the USA, such as Project STAR and Life Skills Training.

- Prevention interventions should probably target a younger age group than that targeted by NE Choices. Age 11, or Year Seven, may be an appropriate starting age for school-based interventions. Furthermore, both young people and parents are more likely to be receptive to school-based activities at this younger age than during secondary school. There are also less stringent demands on school curriculum time at this stage.

8. CONCLUSIONS

- Intervention delivery should be for a minimum of three years, extending beyond this if practicable. Funding or planning constraints that inhibit long-term planning should be overcome where possible. In NE Choices, there was initially no real expectation of delivery to Year Eleven as the Drugs Prevention Initiative, the predecessor of DPAS, was expected to implement an exit strategy for winding up its activities by April 1998. Short-term funding arrangements such as this make it difficult to plan programmes of three or more years duration.

- Interventions should be multi-component and use a range of settings and channels for delivery, including both school and out-of-school. Drugs education that is led and co-ordinated by teachers need not mean that all delivery must be done by teachers or in a classroom setting. It is questionable whether a classroom is a suitable environment for this type of work, and careful use of external delivery agents such as theatre-in-education workers and youth workers can open issues up which cannot easily be addressed by (at least some) teachers. Drama appears to be a particularly appropriate and engaging medium for working with young people, and should be considered as an intervention component.

- Policy and publicity components are not add-ons but should be thoroughly planned and integrated with the core components.

- The needs of vulnerable young people, who may be hard to reach through or disaffected with the formal education system, should also be addressed. Again, this sort of work should be thoroughly planned, and formative or developmental research used to ensure that it is acceptable to all key groups, including schools, parents, Education Welfare, other workers with young people and young people themselves. If schools are to be involved in providing access to vulnerable young people, sensitive discussion and negotiation may be needed to overcome organisational resistance to identifying any of their children as 'vulnerable'.

Funding

- Delivering a prevention trial with adequate strength and integrity requires a realistic amount of funding for management, development, implementation and evaluation. Considerable added value can be brokered in terms of contributions in kind and sponsorship, and these should be sought from a range of sources, including the private sector. Spreading the available resources too thinly – i.e. over too large a number of schools or communities – will undermine programme intensity and delivery. At the same time, however, in a rigorous evaluation trial an intervention must be delivered in a large enough number of sites to allow meaningful analysis of data. Funding levels should therefore accommodate this.

Working in schools

- There are significant challenges to working in schools. Secondary schools may have widespread catchment areas (which may inhibit or restrict work in the school's 'local community'), and the curriculum, especially in the later years of secondary school, is likely to be pressurised. This may limit teachers' willingness to take on board new topics such as drugs prevention. Both these problems are likely to be less salient in primary schools, although the need for adequate support, training and appropriate resource materials for teachers is equally important.

- Commitment of schools to the intervention over its full period (and to the evaluation, if required) is vital. Schools must understand what the requirement will be in terms of classroom time, staff training, and the logistical demands on the school (for example, housing a travelling theatre company for a week or transporting pupils out of the school); equally importantly, they need to see that meaningful benefits will accrue from involvement. A school-based 'product champion' is essential – preferable someone on the senior management team. The intervention team also needs a consistent nominated link person in each school to ensure good communications.

Research

- Interventions should be examined by formative, process and outcome evaluation. Formative research and piloting/pretesting of intervention components ensures that they are acceptable and appropriate, and can be practicably delivered. In NE Choices, nearly all information products and resource materials were pretested with their intended target groups, and both the Year Nine and Year Ten drama workshops were piloted in real life conditions. Enough time should be allowed in the intervention development stage for findings to be fed back and modifications to be made (and pretested further, if required).

- Process evaluation examines delivery of the intervention as it is happening. This plays two important roles: firstly, it can identify if there are any unforeseen problems with delivery or with the format of particular components, allowing modifications to be made to the intervention as needed. Secondly, observation of intervention delivery can provide insights into how the target group is responding – for example, which parts of the intervention they find most interesting, or how group members relate to one another and to the facilitators. These sort of insights help to build up a detailed picture of target group engagement and response.

- Drug use behaviour is the outcome indicator of choice, but outcome evaluation may be reinforced by measuring reasonable proxy indicators such as changes in intentions, knowledge or attitudes, perceptions of risk and so forth. In large-scale evaluations, the school, rather than the individual, should be the unit of analysis.

REFERENCES

Allison KR, Rootman I (1996). Scientific rigor and community participation in health promotion research: are they compatible? *Health Promotion International,* **11**(4): 333-340.

Andreasen AR (1994). Social marketing: definition and domain. *Journal of Marketing and Public Policy.* Spring: 108-114.

Andreasen AR (1995). *Marketing social change: changing behavior to promote health, social development and the environment.* San Francisco: Jossey-Bass.

Bagozzi R (1975). Marketing as exchange. *Journal of Marketing,* **39**: 32-39.

Balch GI, Sutton SM (1997). Keep me posted: A plea for practical evaluation. Chapter 5 in Goldberg ME, Fishbein M, Middlestadt SE (eds), *Social marketing: theoretical and practical perspectives.* Mahwah New Jersey: Lawrence Erlbaum Associates.

Barnard M, Forsyth A, McKeganey N (1996). Levels of drug use among a sample of Scottish schoolchildren. *Drugs: education, prevention and policy,* **3**(1): 81-89.

Blakey V, Pullen E (1991). You don't have to say you love me: An evaluation of a drama-based sex education project for schools. *Health Education Journal,* **50**(4): 161-165.

Bland JM, Kerry SM (1997). Trials randomised in clusters. *British Medical Journal,* 315: 600.

Botvin GJ, Baker E, Dusenbury L, Botvin EM, Diaz T (1995). Long-term follow-up results of a randomized drug abuse prevention trial in a white middle-class population. *JAMA,* **273**(14): 1106-1112.

Botvin GJ, Baker E, Dusenbury L, Tortu S, Botvin EM (1990). Preventing adolescent drug abuse through a multimodal cognitive-behavioural approach: results of a 3-year study. *Journal of Consulting and Clinical Psychology,* **58**(4): 437-446.

Bouman M, Maas L, Kok G (1998). Health education in television entertainment – 'Medisch Centrum West': A Dutch drama serial. *Health Education Research Theory and Practice,* **13**(4): 503-518.

Bucke T, Grace S, Lloyd C (Eds.) *The Integrated Programme: a multi-component drug prevention initiative.* Forthcoming DPAS paper.

Coffield F, Ridley L (1992). Young people and illicit drug use. Middlesbrough: University of Teesside.

Denman S, Davies P, Pearson J and Madeley R (1996). HIV theatre in health education: An evaluation of 'Someone like you'. *Health Education Journal,* **55**(2): 156-164.

Denman S, Pearson J, Moody D, Davis P, Madeley R (1995). Theatre in education on HIV and AIDS: a controlled study of schoolchildren's knowledge and attitudes. *Health Education Journal,* **54**(1): 3-17.

DfEE (Department for Education and Employment) (1995):

- Secondary school performance tables 1995, Gateshead 390. London: Department for Education and Employment.

- Secondary school performance tables 1995, North Tyneside 392. London: Department for Education and Employment.

- Secondary school performance tables 1995, Northumberland 929. London: Department for Education and Employment.

- Secondary school performance tables 1995, South Tyneside 393. London: Department for Education and Employment.

Elder JP, Wildey M, DeMoor C et al (1993). The long-term prevention of tobacco use among junior high school students: classroom and telephone interventions. *American Journal of Public Health*, **83**(9): 1239-1244.

Elder JP, Woodruff SI, Eckhardt L (1994). Participation in a telephone-based tobacco use prevention program for adolescents. *American Journal of Health Promotion*, **9**(2): 92-95.

Ellickson PL, Bell RB, Harrison ER (1993a). Changing adolescent propensities to use drugs: Results from Project ALERT. *Health Education Quarterly*, **20**(2): 227-242.

Ellickson PL, Bell RM, McGuigan K (1993b). Preventing adolescent drug use: long-term results of a junior high program. *American Journal of Public Health*, **83**: 856-861.

Fawcett SB, Lewis RK, Paine-Andrews A, Francisco VT, Richter KP, Williams EL, Copple B (1997). Evaluating community coalitions for prevention of substance abuse: the case of Project Freedom. *Health Education And Behavior*, **24**(6): 812-828.

Flora JA, Lefebvre RC, Murray DM, Stone EJ, Assaf A, Mittelmark MB, Finnegan Jr JR (1993). A community education monitoring system: methods from the Stanford Five-City Project, the Minnesota Heart Health Program and the Pawtucket Heart Health Program. *Health Education Research Theory and Practice*, **8**(1): 81-95.

Flynn BS, Worden JK, Secker-Walker RH, Badger GJ, Geller BM, Costanza MC (1992). Prevention of cigarette smoking through mass media intervention and school programs. *American Journal of Public Health*, **82**(6): 827-834.

Flynn BS, Worden JK, Secker-Walker RH, Pirie P, Badger GJ, Carpenter JH and Geller BM (1994). Mass media and school interventions for cigarette smoking prevention: effects 2 years after completion. *American Journal of Public Health*, **84**(7): 1148-1150.

Gilham SA, Lucas WL, Sivewright D (1997). The impact of drug education and prevention programs: Disparity between impressionistic and empirical assessments. *Evaluation Review*, **21**(5): 589-613.

Gropper M, Liraz Z, Portowicz D, Schindler M (1995). Computer integrated drug prevention: a new approach to teach lower socioeconomic 5th and 6th grade Israeli children to say no to drugs. *Social Work Health Care,* **22**(2): 87-103.

Hastings GB, Haywood A (1991). Social marketing and communication in health promotion. *Health Promotion International,* **6**(2): 135-145.

Hastings GB, Stead M, Eadie D, MacKintosh AM (1997). Towards an integrated research design for social marketing interventions. *Innovations in Social Marketing Conference Proceedings.* Washington DC: AED and others.

Haywood A, Teer P, Stead M, Hastings GB (1993). *Drug misuse and young people. Report for Northern Regional Health Authority, Drugs Prevention Initiative Newcastle, University of Teesside.* Glasgow: University of Strathclyde, Centre for Social Marketing.

Home Office Drugs Prevention Initiative (1998). *Managing a drugs prevention initiative: The experience of NE Choices 1996-98.* Newcastle-upon-Tyne, Northumbria Drugs Prevention Team.

Houston FS, Gassenheimer JB (1987). Marketing and exchange. *Journal of Marketing,* **51**: 3-18.

Jackson M, Stead M, Eadie DR, MacKintosh AM, Hastings GB and Reece J. (2000) *NE Choices process evaluation: Exercise three – report.* Glasgow: University of Strathclyde, Centre for Social Marketing.

Johnson CA, Pentz MA, Weber MD, Dwyer JH, Baer N, MacKinnon DP, Hansen WB (1990). Relative effectiveness of comprehensive community programming for drug abuse prevention with high risk and low risk adolescents. *Journal of Consulting and Clinical Psychology,* **58**(4): 447-456.

Kelder SH, Perry CL, Lytle LA and Klepp KI (1995). Community-wide youth nutrition education: long-term outcomes of the Minnesota Heart Health Program. *Health Education Research,* **10**(2): 119-131.

Kerry SM, Bland JM (1998). Sample size in cluster randomisation. *British Medical Journal,* 316: 549.

Klepp K-I, Tell GS, Vellar OD (1993). Ten-year follow-up of the Oslo Youth Study Smoking Prevention Program. *Preventive Medicine,* **22**: 453-462.

Kotler P, Roberto EL (1989). *Social marketing: strategies for changing public behaviour.* USA: Free Press.

Kotler P, Zaltman G (1971). Social marketing: an approach to planned social change. *Journal of Marketing,* **35**: 3-12.

Lefebvre RC, Doner L, Johnston C, Loughrey K, Balch GI, Sutton S (1995). Use of database marketing and consumer-based health communication in message design: An example from the Office of Cancer Communications' "5 a Day for Better Health" program. Chapter 12 in Maibach E, Parrott RL (eds), *Designing health messages: Approaches from communication theory and public health practice.* Thousand Oaks CA: Sage.

Lefebvre RC, Flora JA (1988). Social marketing and public health intervention. *Health Education Quarterly,* **15**: 299-315.

Miller PMcC, Plant M (1996). Drinking, smoking and illicit drug use among 15 and 16 year olds in the UK. *BMJ*, **313**: 394-7.

Newcombe R, Measham F, Parker H (1995). A survey of drinking and deviant behaviour among 14/15 year olds in North West England. *Addiction Research,* **2**(4): 319-341.

Nutbeam D, Aaro LE (1991). Smoking and pupil attitudes towards school: the implications for health education with young people. Results from the WHO Study of Health Behaviour among Schoolchildren. *Health Education Research: theory and practice,* **6**(4): 415-421.

Nutbeam D, Macaskill P, Smith C, Simpson JM, Catford J (1993a). Evaluation of two school smoking education programmes under normal classroom conditions. *British Medical Journal,* 306: 102-107.

Nutbeam D, Smith C, Moore L, Bauman A (1993b). Warning! School can damage your health: Alienation from school and its impact on health behaviour. *Journal of Paediatric Child Health,* **29**(1): s25-s30.

OPCS (1994). *Postcode sector monitor 1991 census, Newcastle and the North.* CEN91 PSM 1 London: Government Statistical Service.

Orme J, Starkey F (1998). *Evaluation of HPSA/Bristol Old Vic Primary Drug Drama Project 1997/98.* Full report. Bristol: Faculty of Health and Social Care, UWE.

Parker H, Measham F, Aldridge J (1995). *Drugs futures: changing patterns of drug use among English youth. Research Monograph Series.* London: Institute for the Study of Drug Dependence.

Pentz MA (1996). Preventing drug abuse through the community: multicomponent programs make the difference. *National Conference on Drug Abuse Prevention Research: Presentations, Papers and Recommendations – Plenary Session.* Electronic copy.

Pentz MA, Dwyer JH, MacKinnon DP, Flay BR, Hansen WB, Wang EYI, Johnson CA (1989). A multicommunity trial for primary prevention of adolescent drug abuse. *Journal of the American Medical Association,* **261**(22): 3259-3266.

Pentz MA, Mihalic SF, Grotpeter JK (1997). Blueprints for Violence Prevention: Book One – The Midwestern Prevention Project. Series editor DS Elliott. Boulder, Colorado: University of Colorado.

Pentz MA, Valente W (1993). 'Project STAR: A substance abuse prevention campaign in Kansas City'. Chapter 3 in Backer TE and Rogers EM (eds), *Organizational aspects of health communication campaigns: what works?* Newbury Park, CA: Sage.

Perry CL, Kelder SH, Murray DM, Klepp K-I (1992). Community-wide smoking prevention: long-term outcomes of the Minnesota Heart Health Program and the Class of 1989 Study. *American Journal of Public Health,* **82**(9): 1210-1216.

Peterson AV jr, Kealey KA, Mann SL, Marek PM, Sarason IG (2000). Hutchinson Smoking Prevention Project: long-term randomized trial in school-based tobacco use prevention – results on smoking. *Journal of the National Cancer Institute,* **92** (24): 1964-65.

REFERENCES

Ridley L (1995a). *Parents' focus groups: Findings from interviews held with groups of parents from Newcastle.* Middlesbrough: University of Teesside.

Ridley L (1995b). *Social marketing report of focus group interviews with young people aged 13-16 from Scotswood, Newcastle upon Tyne.* Middlesborough: University of Teesside.

Roberts C, Sibbald B (1998). Randomising groups of patients. *British Medical Journal,* 316: 1898.

Stead M, Eadie DR, MacKintosh AM, Reece J and Burns J (1997). *NE Choices process evaluation exercise one – report.* Glasgow: University of Strathclyde, Centre for Social Marketing: September.

Stead M, Jackson M, Eadie DR, MacKintosh AM, Hastings GB and Reece J (1998). *NE Choices process evaluation: exercise 2 – report.* Glasgow: University of Strathclyde, Centre for Social Marketing.

Stead M, MacKintosh AM, Eadie D, Reece J, Burns J, Hastings G (1996). *NE Choices Formative Research Exercise One: refining the year 9 intervention.* Glasgow: University of Strathclyde Centre for Social Marketing.

Stead M, MacKintosh AM, Eadie DR, Hastings GB (2000). *NE Choices: The development of a multi-component drug prevention programme for adolescents. Home Office Drugs Prevention Advisory Service DPAS Paper 4.* London: Home Office. ISBN 1-84082-514-6.

Ukoumunne OC, Gulliford MC, Chinn S, Sterne JAC, Burney PGJ, Donner A (1999). Evaluation of health interventions at area and organisational level. *British Medical Journal,* 319: 376-9.

Wilmott H (1996). Big Chill: An evaluation of a theatre-based drugs education programme for young people at risk. Cambridgeshire County Council.

Wragg J (1990). The longitudinal evaluation of a primary school drug education program: Did it work? *Drug Education Journal of Australia,* **4**(1): 33-44.